LEE BYRNE

THE BYRNE IDENTITY

To

Tim

Best wishes

'Straight away you could tell he was a good player.
Within a couple of years he was being talked about as
the best full back in the world, and rightly so...
I loved playing with him.'
– Shane Williams

'He had that special something that quality rugby players
possess, the ability to make things look easy, to play
with his head up to see what was happening before those
around him knew something was on. It's a privilege to
remain close friends with such a humble, humorous
and all-round good guy.'
– Hugh Williams-Jones

'Lee played sublime rugby that really stood out.
Great players have the ability to slow everything down...
Lee certainly had that ability. A world-class full back with
an exceptional skill-set – sheer class.'
– Jeremy Guscott

LEE BYRNE

THE BYRNE IDENTITY

with Richard Morgan

To Mum, Dad and Andrea,

for all your support and love.

I couldn't have done it without you. x

First impression: 2017

© Copyright Lee Byrne, Richard Morgan and Y Lolfa Cyf., 2017

The publishers wish to acknowledge the support of
Cyngor Llyfrau Cymru

Cover photograph: Dan Morris Photography
Cover design: Y Lolfa

ISBN: 978 1 78461 461 4

Published and printed in Wales
on paper from well-maintained forests by
Y Lolfa Cyf., Talybont, Ceredigion SY24 5HE
website www.ylolfa.com
e-mail ylolfa@ylolfa.com
tel 01970 832 304
fax 832 782

Contents

'Proceed as if success is inevitable.'
– Unknown

Acknowledgements

I would like to thank all my friends – those from my rugby career and the ones I grew up with – who stuck with me in the good times and bad. I'd also like to thank Richard Morgan for his hard work on this book and Steve Quinn who suggested I write it in the first place! Thanks also to the Welsh Books Council, all the team at Y Lolfa, and everyone who helped contribute photos... old and new. A special thanks to my old school mate Dan Morris for the cover photo, to Shane for the foreword and to Jeremy Guscott and Hugh Williams-Jones for their kind comments.

Lee Byrne
September 2017

Foreword

I didn't know much about Lee Byrne before he joined the Ospreys, as he hadn't come up through the age groups like most other players. But all of sudden we heard about this full back who'd signed for the Scarlets and was playing really well. And then, in 2006, he came to the Liberty Stadium.

Straight away you could tell he was a good player. Within a couple of years he was being talked about as the best full back in the world, and rightly so. He was very rarely injured, was gutsy in defence and had a turn of pace. He also had a great kicking game, and was one of the best 15s around under the high ball. Personally, I loved playing with him. He was different to conventional full backs (and I mean that in a nice way!): he loved being out of position and coming into the line. In fact, he did the second bit so well – taking a sharp angle back towards where the ball had come from – that the technique was named after him. I still talk about 'the Byrney line' when I'm coaching kids today!

Like me, Lee wasn't afraid to try things, even when they weren't 100% on. My motto's always been 'if you don't try things, you never know' (in other words don't be afraid to make mistakes) and Lee was always prepared to gamble. 9 times out of 10 it would come off. He'd put in a little chip and chase and, OK, sometimes he'd get clattered. But the next time he'd get the offload in. We made so many scores for each other by reading what the other was about to do and putting him into space. For that reason, I'd probably say that Lee was my all-time favourite full back to play with – we just complemented each other really well.

Off the field, Lee's very sociable, very friendly, and would do anything for you. In other words, he embodies all the values that I respect in a person. At the end of the day, rugby's supposed to be fun. Yes, as professionals we take it seriously – and we always gave 100% in training and on the field – but if you're not having fun it can be a very difficult environment. Lee, Mike Phillips, James Hook and myself were dubbed 'the Fab Four'. Not because of our deeds on the field (although luckily enough, we enjoyed plenty of successes, both as individuals and collectively) but because we hit it off so well. Don't get me wrong, we were as professional as anyone when it came to training and playing... but we were pretty good at celebrating too!

One time in the company of those lads left me out of pocket, though. It was 2011 and we'd just been knocked out of the World Cup in New Zealand. We decided to go out for a few drinks in Auckland as a stress release. We started at breakfast and then headed into town where we found a swish cocktail place. Later, in a drunken haze, we decided to play 'credit card roulette' to decide who'd pick up the tab (which by this point had reached about 800 dollars). Unfortunately my card was pulled out last. A few rounds later the same thing happened, with the same result… and it was still only lunchtime! I think any win bonuses I'd earned during the tournament evaporated that day.

But that's typical of a night out with Byrney – it's always eventful. He was a fantastic player, and is an even better bloke, and a pleasure to know. We'll remain friends for life.

Shane Williams
September 2017

Prologue

My phone rang. The words 'Rob Howley mobile' flashed up on the screen. It was a Saturday evening in November, 2013. I was sitting in a bar opposite the Stade Marcel-Michelin in Clermont, enjoying a glass of red wine with Alex Lapandry, my best mate in France. Earlier that day, we'd beaten Montpellier in the Top 14, and I'd scored two tries. It was my third season in France and I was playing well. Life was good.

I had a sixth sense about the purpose of the call. There'd been a glut of injuries in the Wales squad, and they were short of full-back cover for the following Friday's match, an Autumn International against Tonga at the Millennium Stadium. I showed Alex the screen: 'Byrney, answer it!' he urged. We'd been friends a while, and he knew how desperate I'd been to reclaim my Wales jersey. I hesitated for a moment... then pressed 'decline'.

Why? On the face of it, I should have been delighted to get Howley's call. After all, I hadn't started a Wales game since the World Cup match against Fiji more than two years earlier. This game was my chance. Who knows: I might have won Man of the Match and gone on to get another 60 caps. At the very least I might have added a few more to my tally of 46. And it would have been a chance to prove my doubters wrong, to show that I could still perform on the biggest stage.

This wasn't the first time I'd heard from Howley that autumn: surprising, because I'd barely spoken with him before then since the World Cup in 2011. But one day, out of the blue, he called me about comments I'd made in *The Western Mail* newspaper. A journalist had contacted me to ask about Jonathan Davies' expected move to Clermont the following season. The conversation had lasted about 25 minutes. I waxed lyrical about Clermont: about how much Foxy would enjoy the rugby and the lifestyle. At the very end of our chat, the reporter asked me about my own international future – specifically, whether I thought I had one. Jokingly, I answered: 'I think they've lost my number!' It was a throwaway comment, forgotten as soon as it was said.

The next day, my phone went – it was Rob. He told me my phone number remark was on the back page of the paper, and wanted to know why I'd made it. 'Rob, on my life... I talked about Jonathan Davies for 25 minutes and said that at the end. There was nothing in it.' At no point did he ask me how I was, or how I was getting on at Clermont. Towards the end of the conversation I asked him how he thought I was playing, and what my prospects were of a Wales recall. He said he'd phone me back to discuss it. The call never came.

You may have inferred from the above that I'm not Howley's biggest fan. We'd started working together in

2008 when Warren Gatland brought him into the Wales set-up. He'd overseen my best moments in a Wales shirt, and I rated him as an attack coach. But, in around 2011, cracks started to appear in our relationship. I'd been suffering with a knee injury, and had worked my backside off to make the squad for the World Cup. But when I returned to the training field, I noticed that Howley had a different attitude towards me. I felt he was trying to undermine me, subtly yet insidiously.

At the time Leigh Halfpenny – the man who was to take my full-back jersey – was flavour of the month. 'Great kick, Halfers. Well done, Halfers!' Howley would yell during training. Fair enough, except when I nailed the same kick there'd be stony silence. 'Awesome angle, Halfers!' he'd cry, only to ignore anything decent I did, whilst loudly criticising my mistakes. These were not isolated incidents, but a recurring theme. The pattern became glaringly obvious to my teammates, who'd take the piss out of me about it. 'Byrney!' they'd shout at me, in imitation of Howley and his signature bawl. It was funny – but I was starting to get the impression the top brass didn't want me.

Please don't think I'm whinging here. I appreciate that coaches have a job to do. And I also understand that players have their sell-by date. Naturally, I wouldn't have enjoyed being phased out of the team however he'd done it. But I'd have had more respect for Howley if, as a senior coach, he'd taken me aside and told me what was happening. That was the way Gatland

generally handled things, to be fair. And I didn't mind
being shouted at, either: Shaun Edwards – another
Gatland lieutenant – did it all the time, but I accepted
it because his intentions were good. This was different.
Far from being a strategy to help me improve, it seemed
to me that Howley's constant sniping was part of a
grinding-down process – step by step and day by day
– to get me out of the team. I felt like he was trying to
break me down mentally, to make me give in so they
could justify dropping me.

The snide remarks had started earlier, when he began
passing comment about my social life. As we both lived
in Bridgend and knew many of the same people, it would
often get back to him if I'd been out. 'Good night last
night, Byrney?' or 'Out again on the weekend, Byrney?'
he'd say, in front of the other players. Again, I thought
this was unnecessary. I'd always enjoyed a night out
when the time was right. It had never been a problem
before, but now it seemed as if my social habits were
being used as ammunition against me.

I wasn't the only player he'd pick on using these
tactics, but few would stand up to him. One exception
was Phillsy (Mike Phillips), who once told him where to go.
That kind of edge made Mike a great player, but it wasn't
my style. Instead, I just put up with it and simmered.

By the 2012 Six Nations, I was no longer first choice
in the Wales team. But I was still named in the training
squad. Each week I'd return from France for training.

This was no mean feat: on the Sunday night I'd take a flight from Clermont to Amsterdam then onto Cardiff, before making the return journey in midweek, after the match-day squad had been announced. To make matters worse, the WRU – as part of their cost-cutting measures at the time – were not covering my travel expenses. The boys who'd driven from Swansea or Llanelli weren't happy about this, so imagine how I felt. All the to-ing and fro-ing left me about five or six grand out of pocket (I eventually got a small amount back). At no point did I consider retiring from Wales duty, but it was a long way to come – at my own expense – to hold tackle bags.

So this was the background to the phone call I received that November night in 2013. Eased out of the Wales team; subjected, in my view, to bullying treatment; dragged back and forth to Wales with hardly any compensation for my troubles. For two years, there'd been no communication with the management; but here was a man – a man who I felt had tried to humiliate me in front of my teammates – ringing up and expecting me to come running because he'd clicked his fingers, to be cannon-fodder for a Friday-night game against Tonga.

I excused myself to Alex and checked my voicemail. Rob's message was as I'd expected: 'Byrney, get on the plane. You're starting against Tonga.' I took a moment to reflect, then called him back. It diverted to his voicemail.

'Forget it, Rob,' I said. 'I ain't coming back.'

I never played for Wales again.

CHAPTER 1

Wildmill Boy

I suppose I was an outsider when it came to rugby: someone who emerged from left field, who overcame the odds. Consider the young player nowadays. Talent-spotted from an early age, hothoused in an academy, capped at under-16s, under-18s, and under-20s levels, and put on a 'player-development pathway' all the way to senior honours. Well, that wasn't me. Mine was more an old-fashioned route to the top. A rags-to-riches tale, you might say.

I was born in 1980, and grew up on the Wildmill council estate in Bridgend. It was one of the roughest areas in town, with lots of poverty. My dad, Martin, was a drayman, delivering beer from the brewery to local pubs, an occupation known as 'the fourth emergency service'. First of all he worked for Courage and later Hurns, a Welsh company. Like many in that line of work, he became fond of a drink himself. He and another guy would deliver to the local pubs, taking it in turns to drive while the other had a pint at each stop. On a non-driving day, that meant he might put away about 10 pints, not counting the couple he'd have at the Riverside Tavern on the way home.

Eventually, Dad gave up the booze, and now hasn't touched a drop for five years. His relationship with my mum is so much better as a result. Nowadays they go on holidays – something they never did before – and I sometimes spot them holding hands. It's done wonders for my relationship with him, too. I love him more than ever, and I know he'd do anything for me.

Dad is a Geordie, from Consett near Newcastle, and a sportsman. Like most people from that part of the world, his passion was football, not rugby. He was decent player, too, though his career came to a premature end after he was banned for life for headbutting an opponent. The story followed him to Bridgend, where he acquired the nickname 'The Flying Head.' Perhaps inevitably for the son of a football-loving Geordie, I've always supported Newcastle United. In particular, I worshipped Alan Shearer. Next time you see one of my tries repeated on TV, note the celebration: arm up, index finger pointing skywards. Just like Alan.

Dad met my mum, Lynne, when they were both working in Jersey. Mum – in those days a cleaner – is from Cornelly, and they moved back to the area to get married, setting up home in Bridgend. I was close to her family, particularly her sister, my Aunt Hazel, and her kids Rachel (who's like a sister to me) and Julian. I also admired her brother, my Uncle Andrew. He was a sort of

Peter Pan figure, good-looking and always enjoying life. Julian and I wanted to be like him when we got older.

Aunt Hazel ran pubs (you may notice a theme developing here) and, when mum went to clean them, I'd go along and root around under the cushions for lost coins. It could prove quite lucrative. When Aunt Hazel died in 2011, I was devastated. At the time, I was at the World Cup in New Zealand. I'd known she was ill with cancer, but after I left she deteriorated rapidly and the doctor told her she only had days left. Despite this, she told the family not to inform me, as she didn't want me to come home and miss the tournament. It was only during a routine call home that I found out she'd died. Missing her funeral is one of my greatest regrets.

Ironically, Aunt Hazel needn't have worried about me missing anything in New Zealand. By this point, my relationship with members of the Wales management had soured, and my campaign ended in disappointment. But losing my aunt would have been a massive blow, whatever my fortunes on the field. Her death really affected me, but it wasn't something I felt I could share with the boys. Instead I bottled it up and got pissed – a coping strategy I've tended to rely on over the years.

I have one sister, Sian. Of the two of us, she's definitely got the brains. She went to university before becoming an occupational therapist. We owe everything to Mum and Dad. They didn't have much, but everything they did have they gave to us. As a teenager, I used to dream of one day being able to buy them a nicer house. Luckily, my success in rugby has helped me to achieve that goal: they now live in a new-build home near me, in the Broadlands area of Bridgend. It's great to have them nearby. In the past, it proved pretty handy for the washing, too!

*****

It was rough on the Wildmill Estate, but I had a wonderful childhood. When I was three or four, I started hanging around with a group of older kids, all about four years older than me. Boys like Carl Tozer, Carle Ellis, Marcus Tooze, Mark Florence and his cousin Rhys, Simon Livick, Andrew Smith, Dean Jones, Jonathan Stoker, Gareth Bartlett and Mike Bevan. I'm still friends with them today.

Most of our time was spent playing sport, which wasn't easy since the estate didn't have a playing field. We'd play with any ball we could get our hands on. If there was football on TV we'd play football, if there was cricket we'd play cricket. We'd go golfing with one club and one ball.

Hanging round with those older kids toughened me up. I quickly became known for a fearless (some might say stupid) streak. I'd do diving headers on concrete. We had catching contests with a tennis ball and I'd ask for it to be thrown 30 or 40 feet up. My mate Simon Livick remembers a time when we had a jumping competition off the top of a garage, one of those red-brick buildings with a bitumen roof. It was about 10 feet high, more when you consider the road sloping away from it. I was begging to join in. They let me, but I ended up in plaster with a broken ankle. My mum wasn't pleased and let my mates feel the sharp end of her tongue, but I suppose that early incident showed a bravery in my character which was to serve me well in my later career.

The competitive streak extended to my first experiences in rugby. I was eight when I first started playing at my primary school, St Mary's, but was soon put into the under-11s. The games teacher was a certain Phil Steele, now better known as a pitchside reporter with BBC *Scrum V*. He was pretty strict when he needed to be, and more than once I was on the receiving end of his trademark punishment – a board rubber thrown across the classroom. But 'Mr Stel' (as I once addressed him in a 'thank you' card), was also kind, and one of his favourite teaching methods was to sit at the front of the classroom with a guitar, singing us songs. He also persuaded my mum to let me play rugby with the bigger kids. I suppose she was used to it by then.

As you may have guessed from my misspelling of Mr Steele's name, I struggled with the academic side of things. Later in life, I discovered that I am dyslexic. But, at the time, I was just put in the lowest set alongside kids with other learning difficulties. We were known as 'Kavanagh's kids' after the teacher, Mrs Kavanagh. I was a disruptive pupil, mostly because I couldn't do the work. When the time came for reading aloud in class, I'd deliberately throw a ball of paper or jab someone with my compass so I'd be thrown out. I didn't want to face the humiliation of not being able to read properly in front of the others. Dyslexia was to have implications during my rugby career, though it was problem I managed to hide for many years.

At one point, things got so bad that the powers that be at St Mary's wanted to send me to Oldcastle, the local special school. But Mum fought that tooth and nail, and I was allowed to stay where I was. I'm not criticising the teachers. My reading teacher, Mr Williams, would shake me by the hand every time I got a word right, before giving me 2p! But to be honest, the classroom side of school just passed me by in a blur. It was a different story when the time came for PE, though. I'd always be the first to have my kit on and be ready to go.

St Mary's was a Catholic school and, unlike nearby Litchard where my friends went, not known for its sporting prowess. We'd only play rival Catholic schools, as the other local teams would have hammered us. But I must have been doing something right. One day, the news came that I'd been picked for Bridgend District under-11s, a pretty rare occurrence for a St Mary's boy. It was my first taste of the big time, being part of the team that won the DC Thomas Cup at the old Cardiff Arms Park. Believe it or not, back in those days I was a number 8 – and a fat one at that. I didn't have much pace and never scored a try, but I used to love the big hits. I'd just run around the pitch like a headless chicken, trying to tackle everything in sight. Like I said, I was fearless, which could be another way of saying there wasn't much going on upstairs!

At 12, it was time for secondary school – in my case Archbishop McGrath. My mates went to Brynteg, one of Wales' best-known rugby hotbeds (having produced eight Lions at time of writing). But for me, the rugby side of things at school was non-existent. Instead, I was left to play club rugby on Saturdays for Bridgend Athletic. Anyway, by this stage my mind was on other things, namely the usual teenage distractions of girls and beer. Schoolwork was even less on my radar than it had been before, and I spent much of my time bunking off.

My mother would see me to the bus stop in the mornings, but I'd do a runner before getting on board. Then I'd spend the day hanging round on the train tracks with other kids, smoking roll-up fags and generally talking crap. Mum nearly got into big trouble when the council truancy officer called to report my absences. Later, it became clear that I wasn't going to be entered for any GCSEs. So it was no great surprise to anyone, and a relief to me, when I quit school aged 15 and got a job.

*****

I'd had little pre-school jobs for years, first as a paperboy, then on a milk round. Both of these came to grief, however. I blotted my copybook with Lyndon Young, the milkman, when I drove the float into a wall and knocked it down. My fledgling career may have survived that setback, but for the fact I also had an unfortunate tendency to get the deliveries mixed up. I'd leave silver-top milk at houses where they'd ordered red-top and vice versa, much to the irritation of the customers. Lyndon let me go.

The paper round had gone the same way. George – the somewhat miserable character who ran the local newsagent's – was unimpressed when word reached him that I'd been delivering the papers to the wrong houses. Once again, I received my marching orders. This was a shame: my round was the best paid one. Looking back, I'm sure dyslexia had a lot to do with the problems I was having. Still, it hadn't been a completely wasted effort: every time George wasn't looking, I'd fill up my paper-bag with sweets and chocolates from the shop.

Perhaps with these early difficulties in mind, at 17 I decided to try something more practical: the army. My mate Rhys Florence and I took the train together up to Pirbright for the fitness test. You had to do a one and a half mile run in under 10 minutes 30… I did it in about 6 and a half. It was at that point they took me aside and asked me if I wanted to join the Paras. I was certainly tempted. Rhys did join up and served tours in Bosnia, Northern Ireland and Afghanistan, where he lost some good mates. I opted to return home and took a job stuffing cushions at Creative Upholstery, a local company.

When I was about 18, my dad found me an apprenticeship as a carpenter and joiner with Keith Evans, another nearby firm. They had a contract doing up the Carlton Plaza hotel in Kilburn, London. Before I knew it, I was heading up to the Big Smoke with a group of much older blokes, led by foreman Alan Chilcott and including John Rees, Jonathan Quigley and Paul Braham, to start work. Every Monday morning, they'd pick me up from home at 4 a.m. and we'd drive up to Paddington, where we were staying in digs. On site, my job was to sweep up and pass tools to the workers and generally be a dogsbody. I loved it. All of sudden I was earning £300–400 a week, a king's ransom for a teenager. Instead of wasting my time in school, I was enjoying getting my hands dirty, and the camaraderie of being around my workmates. It did mean I was the butt of a few jokes – being sent out to fetch a glass hammer and the like – but again, being around older guys toughened me up. The social life was amazing. Every night after work we'd go out and drink 8–10 pints. There were also lots of attractive women in the Paddington area from all over the world, and I wasn't shy about doing my bit for international relations. This wasn't long after the end of the Cold War, don't forget!

The Carlton Plaza job lasted about a year. Next, Keith Evans won the contract with restaurant chain Planet Hollywood, who were breaking into the European market at the time. So, for the next six months or so, we travelled all over the continent – to places like Prague,

Munich, Paris and Rome – to fit out the venues. A lot of the time we'd drive to our destination in the van, with me – as the youngest and a non-driver – rattling around in the back with the tools. There were some eye-opening experiences for a youngster, like the time we saw prostitutes touting for business by the roadside in a snowy Czech Republic. But again, the social life was great. The Munich beer festival was a particular highlight. We also had a stint fitting out golf venue The Belfry.

While I'd been working in London, I'd been able to carry on playing for Bridgend Athletic on Saturdays, but that went out of the window while I was overseas. Eventually, I returned home to carry on my carpentry apprenticeship at Bridgend College, but that didn't last. I later worked for Cartrefi Cymru as a Learning Disability Support Provider, where I looked after an 18-year-old autistic boy named Matthew, and then for Morelec, an electrical wholesaler, where I cut cable and drove a forklift truck.

But it was my next move that was to prove pivotal to my future career.

Chapter 2

Turning Pro

Many people have had a positive influence on my career, on and off the field. The support of my family and wife has, of course, been invaluable. In rugby terms, many coaches and players have helped me to hone my game. But, if I had to single out one individual who helped to shape my sporting philosophy – at a crucial moment in my development – it would have to be a guy you probably haven't heard of. His name's Brendan Roach.

I met Brendan when I was working for Edmundson Electrical in Bridgend, where my duties were similar to those at Morelec. We were colleagues, but I soon discovered that we shared a mutual interest – rugby. Brendan was a scrum half and had played at a good level, appearing in Bridgend's European Challenge Cup team in 1998. By the time I met him, he was plying his trade with Tondu in Division 1, the tier below the Premiership.

Despite being over 30 when I met him, Brendan was also known as the fittest man in Bridgend, with an approach to conditioning ahead of its time. In the boot of his car he kept a large tyre. Every morning, before work, he'd be down at the track doing sprints, pulling it behind him. 'This tyre is my best training partner', he told me. 'It never lets me down, and it always turns up.'

Unlike anyone I'd played with before, Brendan also paid close attention to his diet. He was eating foods that I hadn't really bothered with, stuff like porridge in the morning (a far cry from the fry-ups I'd enjoyed on the carpentry jobs) and protein shakes. At lunchtime, he'd warm up jacket potatoes in the microwave round the back of the warehouse, topped with tuna and Greek yoghurt. OK, nothing special by today's standards. But, for the time, Brendan was a man ahead of the curve. Most importantly, it appeared that all the good living and hard work was paying dividends for him on the field. I was keen to learn more.

I was training twice a week with Bridgend Athletic, but I asked Brendan if I could join him for a few extra sessions. Out we'd go at daybreak, to do sprints on the track or up the sand dunes at Merthyr Mawr. All of a sudden, I was taking training and diet seriously. I'd been as thin as a rake during my time at Keith Evans – now I was starting to look and feel like an athlete, and it showed in my performances. I started to get noticed and, for the first time, began to wonder where rugby might take me.

By now, I'd broken into the senior team at Bridgend Athletic and was scoring 10 tries a season. When I started playing for 'the Ath', the full back was a guy called Stuart Morris, a club legend who went on to score about 3,000 points in his career and is still coaching there today. Back then, the head coach was Alan Griffiths, a lovely man who's sadly now died. Alan switched Stuart to 10 to make room for me, and we soon developed an understanding: Stuart would throw a 'miss two' pass and I'd cut through on the angle, often scoring or setting up a try for a teammate.

We were playing in Division 5 Central. But, even at that lowly level, the brown-envelope culture was in full swing. The players would get a 'win bonus' – in my case £25. For more senior figures, it might be £50 or even £75. Up the stairs you'd go to the office, where treasurer Barrie Morris (Stuart's dad, who's also unfortunately passed away) would be sitting, ready to hand you your envelope. Then back down you'd go, to reinvest your bonus at the bar!

On the field, it was rugby in the raw, playing against hard Valleys teams like Nelson, Cefn Coed and Tylorstown. You'd know all about it if you were caught on the bottom of a ruck, and most weeks my body would bear the marks of a good 'shoeing.' But that was nothing compared to the cold. A dank afternoon in some exposed Valleys location was not for the faint hearted, especially when you were standing out in the backs. I showered in my kit afterwards to keep warm.

For all that, I loved the camaraderie. Each Saturday, after a few pints in the club, I'd head into Bridgend with the rest of the team – boys like John Doherty, Steve Hancock, Stuart Morris and also my old Wildmill pal

Carle Ellis – to hit the local nightspots. The Roof, Astons and Bowlers (where a bouncer once threw me down the stairs) were our favourites. In fairness, we often deserved a celebration. During my stint in the senior side, we earned promotion to Division 4 and reached the 2002 Silver Ball Final, where we faced British Steel at the Brewery Field. We lost, but I was named Man of the Match.

I'd turned a few heads with my display, and Newbridge tried to sign me. But, after talking it over with Brendan, I decided to join Tondu instead. This was a big decision at the time, as they and Bridgend Athletic were big local rivals, despite being separated by several divisions. I was also sad to be leaving my mates behind – as I said, the social side of things at 'the Ath' had been great. But Brendan and his training methods had really made an impression on me, and I was ready to take the next step.

The coach at Tondu was Hugh Williams-Jones, the former Wales and Llanelli prop, a connection with West Wales that was soon to prove significant. The club had recently recruited a full back named Stuart Jarman from Merthyr, a goal kicker and very much the marquee signing for the season. But a few strong performances saw me take Stuart's place in the starting line up. At Tondu, I started getting a bit more money – £300 a month – and started to realise that I had a bit of talent. But the path to the higher reaches of the game still seemed frustratingly out of reach.

Unable to see a route to the top in Wales, I decided I'd take advantage of some Scottish ancestry and try out for Scottish Exiles. Ex-Scotland number 8 Eric Peters was running the programme, and he invited me to a trial match in Newbury. But I only played for half an hour, and didn't hear back from them. Given what happened later, it was obviously for the best. I suppose I might have won a few more caps in the blue jersey, but my career wouldn't have touched the heights it did in the red one. And there's no doubt about it: my heart is Welsh.

So, back to Tondu it was. One afternoon, I turned in a good performance against Llandovery, scoring a solo try after catching my own kick ahead. The next day, at training, Huw told me that the Llandovery coach had informed Llanelli's Nigel Davies about my display, adding: 'He (Nigel) wants you to go down to Stradey Park to meet him and Gareth Jenkins.' Naturally, I thought it was a wind-up. Huw assured me it wasn't, and kindly offered to drive me to Llanelli (I still didn't have a car) to meet the famous duo.

At the time, the Scarlets were the main club force in Wales, having reached three Heineken Cup Semi-Finals and been unlucky to not to go a stage further. Gareth made a surprising offer: 'How would you feel about coming down here for pre-season training?' Suddenly, the world of professional rugby seemed within touching distance. Significantly, the next season – 2003/04 – would be the first following the WRU's decision to switch from clubs to regions. Granted, Gareth had only invited me to training: but here was a clear opportunity to stake my claim. It took me about a second to say 'yes'. I spent the journey home wondering what might lie in store for me later that year.

First, there was a season to see out with Tondu. But events soon took an even more outlandish turn. Again, Huw was the bearer of surprising news: 'They've had an injury crisis at Llanelli – they want you to play on Friday night.' Apparently Matt Cardey and Barry Davies had both gone down injured, leaving the Scarlets with no fit full backs for the league game against Pontypridd. I was the next cab off the rank.

A trip to 'The House of Pain' would have been scary at the best of times, but this was Ponty's last top-flight match before the start of regional rugby: the atmosphere at Sardis Road was sure to be intense. Naturally, Gareth wanted me to train with the team before the match so – with the blessing of Edmundson Electrical – I took a few days off work and headed down to Llanelli to meet the squad. My performances in practice that week were average to say the least. Plagued by nerves, I was dropping balls left, right and centre, all watched by the likes of Leigh Davies, Ian Boobyer and Martyn Madden, players I'd grown up watching.

When the night of the game arrived, conditions were filthy, with driving rain and wind. Sardis was packed and the atmosphere emotional, with the supporters turning out in force to pay a reluctant farewell to top-flight rugby.

It was surreal, running out in that atmosphere and lining up opposite players like Neil Jenkins and Paul John. These were top-class internationals who even seemed to have their own jargon: at one point, I overheard Jenks shouting 'worm, worm!' to the players around him. 'Worm', it turned out, was code, issued to signal he was about to put through a grubber kick. But despite my gaffe-prone efforts in training, I was on fire, striking 60 m spiral kicks, and catching and tackling everything. We lost, but I'd more than justified the gamble they'd taken on me, and Gareth upgraded his offer for me to come and train to a three-year development contract.

Just a year before, I'd been playing rugby for fun with my mates at Bridgend Athletic and driving a forklift truck for a living. Now, at the age of 23, I was going to be a professional rugby player.

I was on my way.

CHAPTER 3

Sosban fach

My contract was to train every day with the Scarlets, staying on twice a week for sessions with the Llanelli semi-pro team, who I'd be turning out for on Saturdays. The deal was worth eight grand a year, for three years. I felt like I'd won the lottery. Just walking around in my new kit, proudly displaying the initials 'LB', was a great buzz. I was living the dream, and – after missing out on the opportunities others had enjoyed in age-grade rugby – there was no way I was going to let the chance go begging.

Pre-season training was at the Pembrey Country Park outside Llanelli. I'd spent the summer playing Rugby League for the Bridgend Bulls (alongside the likes of Allan Bateman), on top of which I'd carried on my training with Brendan, so I was in peak condition. So much so, that my new teammates were struggling to live with me. I remember breaking Wayne Proctor's 3K record at the Johnstown running track in Carmarthen (clocking 9 minutes 58 seconds). Later, I was put on the Concept 2 rowing website for the record at the time for speed endurance on the rowing machine, completing eleven

500 m rows, each in 1.26 minutes or under. It was funny – I'd had no frame of reference for what the standards were like in professional rugby – but here I was, a fresh-faced amateur, outrunning and out-lifting all these seasoned pros. I guess much of it was down to hunger. At 23, after my unusual route into the top flight, I had time to make up. I wanted to make every second count.

Feeling fit was hugely important to me. I enjoyed it, but it also gave me a tremendous feeling of confidence. In those early days, I'd often do extra sessions, getting up in the dark on Sundays to do sprints at the sand dunes in Merthyr Mawr. I enjoyed the thought that I was doing things that no other full back would be. They'd be in bed, comfortable with the level they'd reached, whilst I had a burning desire to improve. It was the same when I joined the Ospreys. Sometimes, after training, I'd sneak off to the gym to do extra weights. I soon came to be branded 'the secret trainer'. Guilty as charged, but my relentless approach definitely paid off. I'm certain that talent alone wouldn't have seen me achieve what I did in the game – it took lots of hard work too.

I'll give you an example. Early in my Scarlets days, during the summer break, I went on a lads' trip to Malia in Crete with five mates from home. Like any group of young guys, we were out on the piss every night, getting in at about 7 a.m. After a few hours sleep, the routine was to sit by the pool and recover, before 'happy hour' started at 2 p.m. Except I'd been given a fitness plan by Wayne Proctor, the Scarlets conditioning coach, and no amount of partying was going to stop me from following it. Even if I'd wanted to, he'd have found out – I'd been given a digital heart monitor to record the work I'd done.

2 p.m. would roll around and my mates – Carl, Carle, Rhys, Matthew and Keiran – would get back on the piss at the pool bar with some lads from Liverpool who were staying in our hotel. I'd be running up and down the hill opposite. 'Is your mate alright?' one of the Liverpool lot asked. The Bridgend boys just smiled and shrugged: they were used to my antics by now. But, come 6 p.m., I'd be right back on it with them, drinking flat out. 'Work hard, play hard', that's always been my motto. But when I handed the monitor back to Wayne, it showed I'd 'maxed out' every day for the whole two weeks.

On the field, I was under no illusions that there was still much to learn, but my pre-season performances gave me the confidence that I belonged. I was still living at home, and would get picked up each day from Sarn Services by Ian Boobyer and Gavin Thomas, who'd then spend the journey to Llanelli taking the piss out of me. There were some great characters at the Scarlets at the time – the likes of second-row pair Vernon Cooper and Chris Wyatt, or 'the longs' as they called themselves, and Barry Davies – and we had some cracking nights out. Jumpin' Jaks in Swansea was the destination of choice, with evenings beginning in the VIP area before spilling out into the city. More often than not 'the longs' would be leading the charge, and the banter at training come Monday morning.

Any doubts in my mind about whether professional rugby had a social side had already been dispelled on the pre-season tour to Slovenia. We managed to see off their national team (who, with all due respect, were not known for their rugby prowess) 95-0, complete with an L Byrne hat trick. Then it was time for some proper team bonding. In this case, that involved a session at the bar in the company of Leigh Davies. Leigh was a fantastically talented centre for Llanelli and Wales – the best ball player the country had at the time – and a man who taught me much on the field. He also knew how to enjoy himself after hours.

The day after our win, Gareth Jenkins, another character not shy of a beer or two, took us out to visit the local beach bars. I soon found myself at a table with Leigh and a group of the senior pros, taking part in a drinking came called, unimaginatively, 'Piss yourself'. As you may have guessed, this involved copious drinking... with strictly no comfort breaks allowed. Many of the younger players weren't too keen, but at that stage I was just pleased to share a beer with the likes of Leigh and Scott Quinnell... whatever the rules of engagement.

Leigh was certainly an influence on me in rugby terms, but the man I most enjoyed lining up alongside at Stradey was Regan King. What a player. He got just the one cap for New Zealand – against Wales in 2002 – but in any other country he'd have won a cabinet-full. I've never seen a guy with skills like it. It would be no exaggeration to say that Regan got me into the Wales team. He just had this knack of putting other players into holes, producing a telling pass at just the right moment. Morgan Stoddart – who followed in my footsteps from the Scarlets into the Wales set-up – also benefitted from having Regan playing inside him, as no doubt did many other full backs over the years.

The other thing that singled him out was his unselfishness. I remember a later incident when we were playing together for Clermont Auvergne. It was a Heineken Cup game against Treviso and we were taking them to the cleaners. Regan had broken clear of the defence and could easily have cruised in for a try, but instead he gave the ball to me. I asked him afterwards why he'd done it. 'I just get more joy from watching other players score,' he said. Thanks, Regan!

Perhaps with my promising display at Sardis Road in mind, Gareth gave me a run with the Scarlets at the beginning of the 2003/04 season. I made my regional debut against Munster in September, and scored my first try, against Edinburgh, a month later. Things were going better than I could have imagined. If you'd told me at that point that I was destined to finish the season with a Celtic League-winner's medal around my neck, I'd have been over the moon. In fact, that's just how it worked out. But my journey from warehouse worker to title-clinching rugby star was not as romantic as it sounds. Along the way I suffered a major career setback.

Not long into the season I was picked to play 7s with

an invitational team called the White Hart Marauders at a tournament in Dubai. Gareth gave me his blessing, saying it would be good for my development. I suppose it was my first proper rugby tour (not counting Slovenia), with everything paid for, and I couldn't wait. But just one game in, I tore the anterior cruciate ligament in my knee, ending my season before it had really begun. Obviously I was devastated. Here I was, just a few weeks into my new career, and I'd been set back six months. I returned to Wales for an operation, carried out by surgeon Mark Holt at the Sancta Maria Hospital in Swansea. I had the standard patella graft procedure, where a piece of tendon is used to replace the damaged ligament. No criticism of Mark, but the knee never felt quite right after that. At least it was my right leg, not my main kicking pin.

So, rather than playing and trying to build a name for myself at Stradey, the rest of my season was dedicated to rehab. Luckily (for me, not him), winger Mark Jones was in the same boat, as he'd also done his ACL. It's so much easier doing rehab with someone else, and Mark and I would push each other on in the pool and on the bike. In a cruel twist of fate, he tore the ACL in his other knee during his comeback game. Gareth Jenkins was also very supportive, coming out on bike rides with me to aid my recovery.

What can I say about Gareth? Like most people, I got on well with him. He's obviously a bit of a legend in West Wales, both as a player and as coach for Llanelli, having guided the club to some of their most famous European nights. He's Mr Llanelli, really, having been with the Scarlets all the way through (apart from his ill-fated stint with the Wales team), a sort of Welsh Arsène Wenger. Unlike Arsène, he's now moved 'upstairs', but he was very much a hands-on coach during my time.

Even surgery on his hip wouldn't keep him off the training paddock. There we'd be, running moves on the pitch at Stradey, with Gareth trundling around on a mobility scooter, pointing out some mistake or suggesting improvements. He also had an unusual place for storing his mobile phone – down the front of his pants. More than once, during training, a ringtone would sound, with the incoming caller often Anthony Buchanan, the team manager. Down the front of his tracksuit bottoms Gareth's hand would go: 'Hang on Bucks, I can't speak now, I'm doing line-out practice!'

Like most people, when Gareth's chance as Wales coach came around, I thought it was well deserved. At the time, he was the overwhelmingly-popular choice after all his years of success at Stradey. As we know, things didn't work out for him in the top job, but I wouldn't put that down to just Gareth and his coaches. The players have to take their share of responsibility, especially for the World Cup defeat to Fiji that eventually sealed his fate.

Certainly, his methods were sometimes old-school. The summer tour to Australia in 2007 was a classic example. These days, arriving on Southern Hemisphere soil would no doubt be followed by an early night and a recovery session the next day. But Gareth had other ideas. 'Right boys,' he said in the Arrivals Terminal. 'I've had a word with the doctor, and he says the best way to get over the trip is "jet lag rules". Ten pints, and no spewing.' We needed no second invitation. Straight into the bar it was, where the boys followed doctor's orders to the letter. Well, on the 10 pints part, at least. We weren't quite so successful on the no spewing. The next day was not our most productive on the training field. Dan Kings, who was the team nutritionist at the time, used to measure our pH levels before training to see how hydrated we were. A normal score would have been in the 200s. That day everyone was measuring in the 600–700 range. I was leading the pack on 800-odd. I think that's still a record. All because of 'jet lag rules', and the advice of 'the team doctor'.

Some may disapprove of this behaviour, but all through my career I've been a big believer in the social side of the game. Perhaps it's because I spent my formative years playing amateur rugby rather than being cocooned in the academy system as most promising youngsters are these days. For me, the game was always about enjoyment first and foremost, and part of that meant a few beers when the time was right. The likes of Phillsy (Mike Phillips), Hooky, Shane, Andy Powell, Andrew Bishop and Jonathan Thomas were all cut from the same cloth. And it might surprise you to learn that the New Zealanders, held up by many as the ultimate professionals, like to party with the best of them. Trust me, I spent lots of time with Jerry Collins! But whatever those guys drink, they always front up on the field.

These days, some players' idea of post-match relaxation is a protein shake or a chocolate bar. I'm not judging. There's even more money in the game now, and livelihoods are at stake. Also, in an era where everybody has a camera on their phone, it's easy to get caught out. I was once snapped smoking a cigarette in Cardiff following an international. Within hours, someone had started up a Facebook group entitled 'Lee Byrne loves a fag after a Wales game'. So, given the scrutiny, I can understand why some of the younger boys are a bit wary. But, for me, the pleasure to be had off the field always outweighed the pitfalls. I wouldn't do anything differently if I had my time again.

Just a quick story about Gareth's right-hand man at the Scarlets and for Wales – Nigel Davies, who was also a good guy. Sometimes, Nigel would bring his young son to training and let him practise his kicking in front of the posts afterwards. I remember noticing that the boy was pretty good, kicking the ball quite far for an eight or nine year old. Fast forward 13 years and that lad's doing well for himself: his name's Sam Davies, and he recently made his first start in the Wales number 10 shirt.

*****

Anyway – back to my fledgling career. The 2004/05
season saw me back on the field – albeit with a stiff knee
– and in action for the Llanelli club side. We had a good
season, going on to win the Konica Minolta Cup at the
Millennium Stadium. Scott Quinnell – another Stradey
legend – was doing the coaching. At this point, I was
feeling my way back into the Scarlets set-up, playing on
the wing or sharing full-back duties with Barry Davies,
another left-footer who'd been enjoying a great run of
form – you may remember his famous try at Northampton
in the Heineken Cup, where he slid along the ground
to gather before running in from halfway. At the end of
the season, I had another op to clear out my knee. I
didn't know it at the time, but it was already starting to
disintegrate, and would cause me major problems later.

I started the next season strongly, though, fighting
my way back into the regional side as first choice. But it
was still a surprise when Chief Executive Stuart Gallacher
called me into his office that October. Stuart told me
Wales coach Mike Ruddock had been in touch, saying he
wanted me to come and train with them ahead of the
forthcoming Autumn Series, to 'get some experience'.
Stuart added that he wanted to offer me a new three-year
deal, doubling my money to 16 grand in year one, before
increasing to 20, then 25. Unusually for me, I told him I
wanted to think about it, and took the contract away. To
this day, I'm not sure why – in those days I was prone to
sign anything put in front of me!

Sure enough, the call from Wales came, and down I

went to Sophia Gardens to train with the squad. What I wasn't expecting, given my conversation with Stuart, was what happened next: being named in the squad to play New Zealand in the opener. The result – a 41-3 hammering – was forgettable, my debut, coming on as a 58th minute replacement for Gareth 'Alfie' Thomas, a blur. But, as the excitement of winning my first cap for my country began to sink in, I was struck with the notion that Stuart hadn't been entirely genuine in our conversation. I later found out that there had in fact been no call from Mike Ruddock, but that Stuart – shrewd businessman that he was – had foreseen that Wales might come calling, and tried to sign me up on favourable terms before my market value skyrocketed.

This attempt to tuck me up left a bit of sour taste, but by now other horizons were opening up for me. I'd already been in talks with the Ospreys. Winners of the league title the season before, they were quickly taking over the mantle as Wales' foremost regional side. They'd recently moved into a state-of-the-art new home at the Liberty Stadium and were developing a strong-looking squad. They were also offering a serious pay increase. So, all in all, it wasn't a tough decision to join them after my contract at Stradey ran out.

I saw out the season with the Scarlets, scoring seven tries and helping them to the final of the Anglo-Welsh Cup, but my decision still made me unpopular with some of the fans. They hated me for a few seasons after that. But, mercenary as it may sound, it's a short career and you have to make the most of the opportunities that come your way. And I wouldn't have swapped the experiences I had at the Ospreys for anything.

That said, I want to thank the Scarlets – and Gareth and Nigel in particular – for giving me my chance, and sticking by me when my first season was derailed by injury. Everyone needs a break in professional sport, and they gave me mine – I'll never forget it.

CHAPTER 4

Lair of the Pumas

Before I started with my new region, there was still a season to see out – and not just with the Scarlets: I was getting a run in the national side, too. After my November debut against New Zealand, I started in the loss to South Africa and in the narrow, Nicky Robinson-inspired win over Fiji. Considering I'd spent much of the previous season playing semi-professional rugby, it was all a bit of a whirlwind for me personally. An apt word… given the hurricane that was about to envelop the Welsh game.

Mike Ruddock was in only his second year of coaching Wales, and, given the joyous events of his first, might have been expected to enjoy many more. But despite leading his country to the Grand Slam – our first clean sweep since 1978 – there were murmurings of discontent in the camp. As a 25-year-old kid breaking into the set-up, squad politics were the last thing on my mind. But it was clear that some senior players did not rate Mike, and thought his contribution to the Slam had been overestimated. Many of them were big supporters of Scott Johnson, the attack coach who was already in the set-up when Mike was brought in to replace Steve Hansen.

Matters came to a head in the following Six Nations.
We'd been soundly beaten at Twickenham in the opener
and, as the coach pulled up at the hotel in Richmond,
Mike asked the players not to go out that night. With that,
he got off the bus, at which point a senior player stood
up and told the driver to take us into London anyway.
Poor Mike was left to walk alone into the hotel. Then,
in the build-up to the next game against Scotland, he
was left to face the press solo. The players had decided
to boycott that week's news conference after falling out
with the journalist who'd ghostwritten Gavin Henson's
autobiography. It was clear that Mike had, as they say,
'lost' the dressing room. Given everything that was going
on, perhaps it was no surprise that he decided to quit
after that game.

The public, unaware of the atmosphere in camp, were
stunned by the news. But to those on the inside, even
a newcomer like me, it was clear all was not well. As
I say, I had no problem with Mike. If anything, I owed
him one for giving me my chance. Some years later he
messaged me and told me it had been an honour to give
me my first cap. But some of the more experienced boys
clearly weren't behind him. It was a great shame for
Mike – a decent man who'd come in and, by all accounts,
contributed plenty to Wales' Grand Slam campaign. For
him to leave so soon after that didn't only look strange: it
came to be seen as a textbook example of Welsh rugby's
tendency to shoot itself in the foot.

With all the off-field turmoil, it was no surprise that

we slumped to a heavy defeat in Ireland, followed by a
home draw against Italy and a narrow loss to that year's
champions, France. I'd started all three games, though,
and was named by Gareth Jenkins – who'd by now taken
over the reins as head coach – for the summer tour to
Argentina.

That was a memorable trip in more ways than one. On
a personal note, it's where I scored my first international
try, rounding Juan Martín Hernández in the second-
test defeat at Buenos Aires. It was also the most exotic
rugby culture I'd experienced. The first test was played
at Puerto Madryn in Patagonia, a city that, thanks to
the settlers of the nineteenth century, boasts a thriving
Welsh-language community. I was amazed to find little
kids running up to me and speaking Welsh. As a non-
speaker, I felt a little embarrassed that I couldn't reply
in kind. Thankfully, we had a sizeable contingent in the
party who could manage a conversation in the native
tongue, although the locals were taken aback by the
identity of one of them. It may not surprise YOU to learn
that Nathan Brew speaks Welsh, but that couldn't be
said for the people of Puerto Madryn. I guess they just
weren't used to people of a non-white or South American
ethnicity. So, when Nathan took the stage at the post-
test function and started spouting fluent Welsh, there
were more than a few startled expressions... much to the
amusement of the rest of the squad.

We had no difficulty in understanding the locals on
match day, though. The word 'hostile' would best sum

it up. In fact, it was by far the most aggressive, intense atmosphere I experienced in my career. The local fans (I didn't spot too many Welsh sympathisers, despite the language connection) were penned in behind cages – the sort they used to have at football grounds – which they shook violently. The noise was ear-splitting. It's how I imagine the atmosphere is at the home of Galatasaray, the Turkish football team. As full back, I spent much of my time alone in the back field, and I was absolutely shitting myself.

The fact we were doing well in the match didn't help. This was the game where Alun Wyn Jones, Ian Evans and James Hook all made their debuts, with the latter two both scoring excellent tries. Now 'Ianto' is a great character, a good tourist and a real wind-up merchant, but I'm not sure we were thanking him for stoking the fires that day. He'd just scored a superb interception try, and decided to wind up the baying mob in the stands by tauntingly cupping his hand to his ear. The place erupted. There were toilet rolls flying onto the pitch, and I thought the cages were going to come down. All things considered, maybe it was for the best that we ended up slipping to a narrow, 27-25 defeat!

As the score suggests, we could have won that game. I'd made a few defensive mistakes but kept my place for the next test at Vélez Sarsfield in Buenos Aires, where I scored my first Wales try... although we lost the game 45-27. But, that defeat and the unfriendly Puerto Madryn crowd aside, it had been a great tour. The people were warm and welcoming, and the food fantastic. I'd like to go back someday.

The trip did prove a bit expensive for one of the boys, though, after he was hit with a big fine for kicking down the door to the team room. Team Manager Alan Phillips was none too pleased when the hotel informed him about the damage, and the culprit was fined most of his tour fee. I bet he wished he'd knocked for a bit longer.

All in all, it had been a memorable end to a memorable season. Now I had a new challenge to look forward to, with a new region. Life as an Osprey was about to begin.

CHAPTER 5

Welcome to Ospreylia

'How big's your cock?' Not a common first question at a job interview, I'd imagine. But this was the opening enquiry made of me by Lyn Jones, head coach at the Ospreys, my new regional team for the 2006/07 season. It was the kind of offbeat behaviour I'd soon learn to expect from Lyn, one of the most innovative – but maddest – coaches Wales has ever produced. The scene was Mike Cuddy's headquarters. Facing me across the table were Mike – the owner of the Ospreys – Lyn, and assistant coach Sean Holley. It was 2005, and I was still under contract at the Scarlets, but after ten minutes with those three, I knew that Swansea would be the next stop on my rugby journey.

If the Scarlets had dominated Welsh rugby for the previous decade, by now there was a sense that power was shifting eastwards. Mike had ploughed money into the new Neath-Swansea venture – heralded, with some justification, as the 'one true region' by its fans – and the future seemed full of possibility. The team had moved to the Liberty Stadium, the brand new home they shared with Swansea City, at the start of that season. The facilities were world class, with a cutting-edge hybrid playing surface and fantastic gym. The squad, filled with top Welsh talent like Shane Williams and Ryan Jones, and supplemented by overseas stars such as Filo Tiatia and Stefan Terblanche, looked formidable. And the money was welcome, too. I suddenly went from £8,000 a year at the Scarlets to £50,000 with the Ospreys, a quantum leap in terms of earnings. I was now a professional player with a salary to match.

That said, any prospect of me getting above myself was quickly put to bed in my first training session with my new teammates. We were warming up with some touch rugby when Alun Wyn Jones – who I knew from the Wales tour to Argentina – picked me up and upended me onto the ground. Incensed, I jumped to my feet and asked him what he thought he was doing... or something along those lines. In response, he just laughed and pushed me away. Welcome to Ospreylia.

I shouldn't have been surprised. Alun Wyn is definitely one of the most competitive people I've played with. Sometimes we'd do sprints in training, and he'd be dipping at the line, trying to finish ahead of everyone. On the pitch, he was an absolute warrior. Off it, he's a really good guy – surprisingly shy, certainly different to the abrasive image he sometimes projects in front of the media. He likes to do his talking on the pitch, but I think people will see a different side to him when he retires.

I'm sure the edge brought by Alun Wyn and others was

part of our success, and it was great to be a part of it. I scored a try on debut against Edinburgh in the Magners League. Another notable win came in November, when we beat Australia to become the first regional team to topple a touring international side. Later that season we reached the final of the Anglo-Welsh Cup, only to lose to Leicester (a defeat we avenged the following year by beating the Tigers to lift the trophy), before finishing as league champions.

Behind it all was Lyn. Crazy, yes, but a tactical genius. We had a particular playing style, but within that, Lyn made sure we had plenty of tricks to call on. One move he pioneered was the so-called 'Andy Allen', named after a former Wales lock whom he didn't rate. It was a line-out play, involving a throw to the second rows, who would then split to allow Mike Phillips to run between them. We practised and practised before trying it out in a league game. Sure enough, it worked a treat, and Mike ran through to score.

That same strange sense of humour I'd witnessed at my interview was never far away. It often emerged during video-analysis sessions. Lyn would stand there in front of the group, remote control in hand, dissecting some aspect of play or another. Suddenly he'd pause and rewind the video, as if to pick out a particular incident, only to point to a player who'd ended up with an opponent sitting on his face in a ruck. 'Hmm,' he'd say. 'You enjoyed that, didn't you?'

Then there was the time after we'd beaten Border Reivers to win the league title. Lyn came into the dressing room and went up to our lock Brent Cockbain, who was having a shower. He smiled warmly and extended his hand, as if to congratulate Brent on his performance. The player reciprocated, only for Lyn to lower his arm and shake Brent by an entirely different part of his anatomy. Understandably, our adopted Aussie looked a little taken aback.

Sometimes, if Lyn felt we didn't need to do any more work, he'd just tell us to fuck off home. Later, when I teamed up with him again at the Dragons, he was a different character, and under a lot more pressure. He was coaching a struggling team, and with far fewer resources at his disposal. At the Ospreys, where he had a considerable depth of talent to choose from, he was much more relaxed.

Scott Johnson – former skills coach with Wales – took over from Lyn as head honcho. As Director of Coaching, he didn't have much to do with the hands-on side of things, and we were never close. I always got on well with Sean Holley, though, and with then forwards coach Jonathan Humphreys, who became my unlikely kicking buddy. Before matches he'd stand down one end of the field while I'd punt balls at him, which he'd return – badly. Well, what do you expect from a former hooker? Except for this one time at Kingsholm, when for once in his life Humph caught the ball a peach, dispatching a perfect spiral kick into 'the Shed' (the fabled home stand), where it spectacularly smashed a tray of beers out of an unfortunate woman's hands.

My preferred kicking style was always the old-fashioned spiral technique. More recently the 'end over end' approach has been more in vogue (possibly due to the influx of Wallaby coaches with their Aussie Rules influences), but I always found I could get more range with the spiral. It helped that I was able to get plenty of leverage on my kicks. If you look back at videos, you'll see I had a very high follow through, which helped me to get massive distances. The only time I had trouble was at the end of my career at the Dragons, when the Pro12 started using Rhino balls. Previously I'd been used to the Gilbert or Adidas. I just couldn't catch the Rhino properly. It was a bit embarrassing, really. There I was at training, the seasoned pro (and captain) but unable to reproduce my signature siege-gun kicks. Give me a good old-fashioned Gilbert any day.

It's a little-known fact that I also kicked from the tee during my professional career. OK, not often: only the once, in fact. It was against Connacht in a league match back in 2007. Shaun Connor had gone off, so the kicking duties passed to yours truly. The record shows that I duly notched up a tally of 10 points (two penalties and two conversions), mostly from in front of the posts. I enjoyed the experience, though, and I often wonder how my career would have panned out if I'd had goal kicking in my arsenal. I reckon I'd have won more than the 46 caps, that's for sure. But in international rugby these days you have to be up around the 90% success rate to make it as a kicker. With all the practice required, it's also a pretty lonely business, and I take my hat off to the likes of Leigh Halfpenny and Jonny Wilkinson for the dedication they show to their craft.

*****

We had plenty of success on the field, but we also enjoyed our social life at the Ospreys. In fact, I've never played with a 'looser' bunch. My suit-carrier was a constant companion in the dressing room. After the game, I'd hang up the suit I'd worn to the ground and get my glad rags on, ready for a night on the tiles. Nikki Walker, our Scottish wing, joked that the suit-carrier was a more important accessory than my gumshield! Life in Swansea was a bit of a culture shock for Nikki (or 'the creature', as we called him, after Bill McLaren used the term to describe him on TV). He'd started his career at Hawick in the Scottish borders, a town famous for its Pringle knitwear and sandstone buildings: a night out on Wind Street was a bit of an eye-opener for him.

He should have had an idea of what was coming his way, mind, after playing for Borders against us in 2006. Some way into the game, the Borders prop popped up from a scrum, with an appalled expression on his face. 'Fucking hell, Nikki', he shouted to 'the creature', who was standing nearby. 'I can't scrummage against this guy any more – he's buzzing of booze!' The 'guy' he was referring to was Andrew Millward, our tight-head. Andrew enjoyed his red wine and cheese, and it appeared he'd been partaking of both the night before. Such refined habits clearly didn't do him any harm: since hanging up his boots, he's gone on to become Ospreys General Manager.

Nikki was a real specimen of a man. On the opposite wing we had a player who was smaller in stature, but with a giant reputation: Shane Williams.

I loved playing with Shane. I remember watching him for Neath when I was younger and thinking, 'imagine having the talent he's got.' He was phenomenal, running round in his baggy jersey and scoring these magic tries. People say Shane and I had a telepathic understanding. It may have looked that way, but most of it was down to work rate. Knowing he could conjure something from nothing, I would always make sure to be on his shoulder in case he made a half-break. Look back at the videos and you'll see that nine times out of ten I'd make a run and it would come to nothing. But that tenth time, he'd know I'd be there and he'd put me through. It was the same for Wales – look at the try I scored against Australia when we beat them in 2008. Shane got the ball at first receiver and, being Shane, attracted two or three defenders, before popping the pass up as I came through on the angle. Often you'd hear shouts of 'Byrney line!' in training for the Ospreys or Wales, the 'Byrney line' being the sharp angle I'd take entering the movement. That

Australia try was a classic example of the Byrney line in practice.

Shane was untouchable in 2008, a deserved winner of the IRB World Player of the Year Award. The try he scored against France to seal the Grand Slam, where he hacked a loose ball through and gathered it at full tilt... I'm convinced no one else on the planet could have done it. He liked nothing better than to run at people one-on-one (especially the big men), and he could make you look silly. Like George Best, he'd give opponents twisted blood. The secret was how he'd run straight at you, sidestepping only at the last second, to leave the would-be tackler flailing at thin air. The way he signed off his careers for Wales and Ospreys (with tries in each case) was typical Shane. And you can't begrudge him any of the plaudits. Once written off as too small, no one worked harder to overcome the odds and prove the doubters wrong.

At the Ospreys, Shane and I, along with Hooky and Phillsy (Mike Phillips), formed the 'Fab Four', a moniker made up by Ryan Jones, based mostly on the fact we liked hanging out with each other. Just four dull bastards sitting round talking shit. Hooky would be going on about *Home Alone*, his favourite film. Mike would burst in and tell us for the umpteenth time that he'd found 'the one', only to notice by the next week that 'the one' had a hair on her toe or ate funny. We'd take the piss out of Shane for his size, obviously. They picked on me for being a secret trainer.

We also shared a passion for male grooming. Maybe it was Gavin Henson who'd set the trend on that score, actually – using fake tan and getting his body hair lasered – but the 'Fab Four' were quick to follow in Gav's footsteps, and others followed us. St. Tropez made a killing off us. Even Tom Shanklin started looking orange at one point! My pre-game ritual normally included half an hour on the sunbed followed by a spot of hair removal. Such behaviour might make the purist frown. But there was definitely a psychological element to it as far as we were concerned. 'Look good, feel good, play good' – that's what we used to say. And I definitely felt like I played better after a good shave and a nice tan.

I guess people look back at the Ospreys team of those years and wonder why we never did better in the Heineken Cup, given the talent at the region. After all, we were christened 'the *galácticos'* by the press (after the great Real Madrid football team of the noughties.) We reached three quarter-finals in my time at the region, the first in 2008. Fresh from an Ospreys-inspired Grand Slam (there'd been 13 of us in the starting team against England), we were strong favourites to beat Saracens at Vicarage Road, especially since we'd smashed them in the EDF Cup the previous month. The game was 3 weeks after the Six Nations ended, so – given the tight turnaround and the sheer number of Wales players at the Ospreys – Lyn decided that we should play like the national team. That meant adopting 'Warrenball', as it came to be known: sucking in defenders on the short side, before spreading the ball and utilising the full width of the pitch. Width had worked well when we dominated Sarries at the Millennium Stadium that March. But, on the much narrower Vicarage Road pitch, the tactics came to grief. Every time the ball went out, we'd find defenders lining up to smash us. The English side had worked us out, and we lost 18-12.

I suppose an inability to come up with a Plan B is a problem for Welsh teams, including the national side. When I was involved, Gatland would be forever telling us that we were fitter and stronger than the opposition. 'Keep going and you'll break them down,' he'd say. And obviously we've had success with that approach, with two Grand Slams, a Championship and a World Cup semi-final appearance. But, in the end, teams work out what you're trying to do, so the challenge becomes how to develop your game. With the Wales team, I sometimes felt like we had 100 calls but no idea about where to go when the game plan wasn't working. That's where New Zealand and Australia come into their own, with their ability to change things up and play what's in front of them.

Look at the skills in the All Blacks team. The likes of Dane Coles and Brodie Retallick may be front five forwards, but could probably do a decent job at outside half! All their players can give and take a pass, while I'm not sure all 15 in the Welsh team would feel comfortable stepping in as, say, an emergency scrum half. It's ironic, really, as Wales have traditionally been considered one of the more skilful teams. But the All Blacks have stolen a march in that respect. It all starts in the schools and with the way the youngsters are coached to play the game.

*****

Back to the Ospreys. I didn't play in our last 8 defeat to Munster in 2009 due to injury. But I was back on board for what turned out to be our best shot at winning the cup in 2009/10. Incidentally, that campaign saw me caught up in a bizarre incident during our group match against Leicester, where we briefly played with 16 men. I'd gone off for treatment and Scott Johnson sent on a message for Sonny Parker, warming up on the Liberty Stadium touchline, to replace me. Not long after, I was ready to retake the field, but the message that I was coming back on never got through to the fourth official. Just as I reappeared, Leicester had a scrum deep in our half, with a two-to-one advantage on the short side. I filled the hole and was able to snuff out an attack that could well have ended in a try. It was a decisive moment in a pivotal match, which saw us go through to the quarters at the Tigers' expense.

Understandably, they were furious. The region was fined €25,000 and I was suspended for two weeks, which would have ruled me out of Wales' Six Nations opener against England. In the end, my part of the punishment was overturned on appeal, but it was still an awkward incident for the Ospreys, and especially our then team manager Dani Delamere, who was left in tears after a dressing down from referee Alan Lewis.

Still, our stroke of good fortune sealed our spot in the quarter-final, this time against Biarritz in the Spanish city of San Sebastian. To my mind, this was the year we really should have won the Heineken Cup. We would have faced Munster in the semi-final in Cardiff, then Toulouse in Paris: a tough ask, but we'd have fancied ourselves. As it was, we lost by just one point in a Basque Country thriller. Early on, Shane Williams and I were left for dead by American speedster Takudzwa Ngwenya, who scorched home from about 70 m. But we played some great rugby to get ourselves back into it, outscoring the Frenchmen by three tries to two and refusing to be intimidated by the partisan home support. I scored our second following a vintage backs move: after the break, Nikki Walker's try put us within touching distance of a famous win. But Dan Biggar's drop goal at the death went narrowly wide, and it finished 28-27.

It was gutting. We felt so deflated afterwards, knowing that we'd let slip our best opportunity to win the biggest title in the club game. So it proved. Neither the Ospreys, nor any other Welsh side for that matter, have progressed further in the competition since. Unless an Arab sheikh comes in and buys one of the regions, I don't see that changing any time soon – the English and French clubs are just too rich and powerful.

There was no time to dwell on the disappointment,

however. On the following Tuesday, we had a crucial Magners League match against Ulster in Belfast. Lose, and we looked set to miss out on the play-offs... which really would have been an unacceptable result for such a talented squad. With another away fixture, v. Leinster at the RDS, slated for the Friday, there was no point in returning to Wales following the trip to Ravenhill. So Sean Holley proposed an 'old-school' mini-tour, staying in Ireland for the week to train and do a bit of team bonding. I guess the idea was to get the Biarritz disappointment out of our system.

The week started on a winning note, as we beat Ulster with almost an identical side to the one that had lost out against Biarritz three days before. In doing so, we'd made sure of our place in the play-offs. Whether it was relief at that, a delayed reaction to the Biarritz result, or a bit of both, it felt like the pressure had been released. And with three days till the next match, that meant it was time for the mother of all piss-ups.

Unfortunately, the evening's revelries coincided with a wedding reception at the hotel – which is where things started getting out of hand. The poor bride narrowly missed being hit by a flying glass. There were one or two scuffles. Andrew Bishop – not the biggest bloke in the squad but definitely the hardest – laid a couple of teammates out. Someone shat the bed. We were still going strong the next morning when Mike Cuddy departed the hotel in his helicopter. I was sitting on the terrace at the hotel with the other boys, fag and beer in hand, waving him off. Soon afterwards the Ulster squad arrived (they used the hotel facilities) to debrief the previous night's game, accompanied by their coach David Humphreys. 'You're up early, boys,' he said, cheerily. 'Pool recovery is it?' Then he came closer and noticed the table full of half-finished pints and vodka shots. It was 8 a.m.

A few hours later, Sean called an emergency team meeting. He had a face like thunder as he took us to task for what, in truth, had been some pretty poor behaviour. Sean ranted about how disgracefully we'd acted, and how the hotel management were threatening to kick us out and never host us again. After about ten minutes of this diatribe, Sean – face bright red – paused and said, 'Do you notice anything different about me this morning?' Hooky tentatively put his hand up. 'Your belt buckle, Sean?' he asked, pointing to the new Osprey motif on the coach's midsection, a recent addition to the region's fashion line. Funnily enough, this was in fact exactly what Sean had in mind: he was trying to make a point about the importance of squad unity. But Hooky's comment sounded so random that we all fell about laughing.

With another 24 hours to kill in Belfast, and determined to avoid a repeat of the previous evening, the management decided to take us on a tour of the city's historic spots. Mike McGurn, our Ulster-born fitness coach, guided us around areas linked with Belfast's troubled past, where we posed for photos in front of the famous murals, and even visited a Republican pub. That was interesting, though I'm not sure what the regulars made of a bunch of polo shirt wearing, alco-pop drinking Welsh rugby players with fake tans.

Perhaps George Best – Belfast's most famous son – would have appreciated where we were coming from. We hoped so, as a visit to Bestie's grave was the next item on the itinerary. Off the 'Fab Four' went, to pay our respects at the final resting place of the great man (he had, after all, once been christened the 'Fifth Beatle'). Afterwards, we decided to pay tribute to George in fitting manner – with a few Guinnesses. Only a few mind. About six pints later (or half a dozen Vodka Ices, in the case of Hooky), we headed back to base. After all, the next day we were due in Dublin to get ready for the Leinster game.

All things considered, a 20-16 defeat wasn't a bad effort. There were a few sore heads and bodies when we finally decamped back to Wales (a journey made by road and sea, with air travel in lockdown due to the Icelandic 'ash cloud' of that year) and training felt a little flat on the Monday. I seem to recall withdrawing from the session with a 'hamstring twinge.' But although things in Belfast had got a bit out of control, that trip actually made us much stronger. We'd had a great laugh, and in my experience that's better than all the training in the world when it comes to bringing a group together. Sometimes there's nothing like time shared together over a few beers to build that elusive quality, team spirit – an ideal much talked about but difficult to achieve, and all too easy to pick apart in the tough times if the underlying relationships are weak.

We went from strength to strength after that. We saw off Glasgow in the semi-final at the Liberty, and were in fine fettle for the final against Leinster, again at the RDS. We'd had a few good battles with the Irish province over the years, but on this occasion we definitely had the better of them. Everyone played well. I was on the end of a pass from Hooky to score the second of our tries, and was awarded Man of the Match in a 17-12 win. Afterwards it was straight back to Cardiff, where we hit the bright lights, winners' medals around our necks.

Looking back, I suppose it was the end of a golden era for Ospreys rugby. From 2011, with the region shedding many of its best players amid cost-cutting measures, the club was no longer able to compete consistently on the biggest stage (although they did brilliantly to win the league again in 2012). As a group of players and coaches, we had much to be proud of. Yes, we'd come up short in Europe. But with an Anglo-Welsh trophy win and now two league titles in four seasons, we'd proved ourselves to be one of the best teams in Britain.

At time of writing, the Ospreys are going through a transitional phase, with the Scarlets once again the premier side in Wales. But it'll take a big injection of cash for any of our regions to succeed on the European stage. Hopefully – with the WRU gradually taking a bigger role in the running of the professional game – it won't be too long before see a Welsh team on the winners' podium.

CHAPTER 6

Gatland arrives

I guess lots of players can point to a pivotal incident in their career, a *Sliding Doors* moment where, had things gone another way, everything might have worked out differently. It could be an injury, a particular match, or just a particular bit of play. For me, that moment came on 2 February 2008, the day Wales played England at Twickenham in the Six Nations Championship. There were 67 minutes on the clock, and I scored a try that not only changed the course of the match, but also the tournament, and, quite possibly, my whole career.

I remember the moment vividly. As I slid over the line, I looked up to see about 100 flashbulbs going off. You may recall the photo: my arms aloft in celebration, teammates rushing in to mob me, Jonny Wilkinson chasing me down forlornly in the background. It was a simple score – about a 10 m run-in – but a massive moment in my career. I hadn't played particularly well in the game up till then. If I hadn't scored, who knows? I may never have been picked for Wales again. As it was, getting that try – at that moment, in that game – gave me the confidence to kick on.

*****

I played some of my best rugby at the Ospreys, but the move didn't produce an instant upturn in my international fortunes. In fact, after a decent start to my Wales career, the 2006/07 season saw me pushed to the fringes. Following the previous summer's trip to Argentina, I made just the one outing the following autumn, against the Pacific Islanders, and didn't feature at all in the following Six Nations. Kevin Morgan and Gareth 'Alfie' Thomas were both ahead of me in the pecking order at this point, so it was no great surprise when Nigel Davies, Wales assistant coach at the time, took me aside that summer and told me that I wouldn't be going to the World Cup in France.

I was disappointed, but I can't say I was shocked. I hadn't really been part of their plans the previous season, so I'd become more or less resigned to not being included. It didn't help my case that I'd played in the record pre-tournament warm-up hammering by England. That was the match, you may remember, when their number 8, Nick Easter, scored four tries as we suffered a 62-5 defeat. My main memory of the afternoon was successfully tackling Jason Robinson. With the flying winger through and just me to beat, I was shitting myself as he hurtled towards me, but I managed to stop him... not that it did me much good.

Going into the game I'd assumed that – while the core of the squad was already picked – there might be a few places up for grabs. Hearing Gareth talk afterwards, though, that was clearly no longer the case. A few days later, Nigel gave me the bad news at our Vale of Glamorgan HQ. Some people say he and Gareth didn't want me because of the way I'd left the Scarlets, but I never had that impression. And, as things turned out, it was probably a blessing in disguise that I didn't go.

Obviously, I can't say what went wrong during that ill-fated World Cup campaign, as I wasn't there. But I did feel for Gareth and the way things ended for him. I suppose he and Nige had to carry the can for our group-stage exit to Fiji, but it was sad nonetheless to hear about the manner of Gareth's departure. He'd been given the sack the day after the game in Nantes, before the squad made their journey back to Wales. Knowing there'd be a sizeable press contingent awaiting his return to the Vale Hotel, Gareth opted to slip off the coach before it drove into the resort. He then sloped off into the distance, duty-free Toblerone in hand. A sad ending for a man who'd spent his whole coaching career dreaming of leading his country. I could have cried for him, wondering what thoughts were going through his mind as he made that lonely walk back to his car.

*****

For me, there were much better times just around the corner. That December, the WRU announced that Wasps coach Warren Gatland had been appointed to lead Wales, and the following month I was named in the New Zealander's Six Nations squad. The first thing Gatland said was that, as he didn't know us or have any history with us, he was going to pick purely on what he saw. He was starting from a blank sheet.

Immediately, we were struck by the intensity of training. From the off, he told us that our fitness was light years behind the All Blacks – he'd be spending the next four years getting us into shape. Sessions were short and sharp. Under Gareth, we'd never know how long a session would be – or rather, we had a rough idea, but training could easily overrun by half an hour. When Warren said we'd train for 45 minutes, we did just that – and not a second longer. He'd have a stopwatch, and after the allotted time passed he'd blow his whistle and that would be that. It didn't matter if someone had dropped a ball in the last movement, he'd tell us: 'You've had your chance, the 45 minutes is up.' This was actually a masterful piece of psychology, as it would leave us desperate to come back and start strongly next time.

Sam Warburton aside, I never knew Gats to get really close to any of the players. He'd crack the odd joke, but he made sure to keep his distance, which is as it should be. He also introduced a culture of constructive criticism. In video analysis sessions on the Monday following a game, he wouldn't flinch from 'naming and shaming' those who'd made a mistake. It wasn't fun if you were on the receiving end, but I thought it was fair enough: you need that honesty. He was only trying to make us better, after all, and everyone was treated the same way. It did mean there was no hiding place, though. If you'd had a shit game, you'd know all about it come Monday morning.

Along with Warren came the rest of his lieutenants from Wasps – Rob Howley, fitness coach Craig White, and Shaun Edwards. Shaun was a loose cannon for all the right reasons, and I liked him from the start. I saw him, a Northerner, as someone from a similar working-class background to myself, and he became a good mentor. Early on, Shaun gave me a tip – a rugby-league technique – that I went on to use for the rest of my career: follow the ball. Previously when defending, I'd position myself in the middle of the field. On Shaun's advice I started following the ball – so if the opposition winger had it, or the centre, or the number 10, I'd be in line with that player. It was a simple but effective tactic, and Shaun believed in it religiously. If the video footage revealed I'd been out of position – say I'd been slow getting up after a tackle – he'd bawl me out in front of the squad: 'Fucking hell, Byrney! Why weren't you following the fucking ball?' He wouldn't hold back, but again, I never took the criticism personally. He'd always say: 'If I shout at you, it means I rate you. If I don't talk to you, you're in trouble, because that means I think you're shit.' If that was true, I'd take the bollocking any day!

Shaun also realised that I lacked confidence (partly due to my dyslexia). So, to help me stay calm before matches, he'd lend me books to read. Mostly sports biographies – nothing too heavy, and half the time I'd just be looking at the pictures, ha ha – but they helped me to stay on top of my nerves.

Within a couple of weeks, the new methods were already yielding results. But our opening assignment remained an intimidating one: England at Twickenham, a fixture we hadn't won since 1988. And, as we ran off at half time trailing 16-6, it didn't look like the losing sequence was about to end, despite Huw Bennett's brilliant, try-saving tackle on English winger Paul Sackey. But then came the second half, or rather, the last 15 minutes of it. We'd clawed our way back to 19-12, and England were starting to look a bit ragged. Then Hooky – playing in his favoured position of number 10 – conjured a piece of magic, embarking on a jinking run to beat three defenders and put me in. His conversion left the scores tied. Moments later, Mike crossed in the same corner after charging down Balshaw's clearance. Again, Hooky converted from the touchline, and we held on for a 26-19 win. It was quite a thing to be on the pitch at the final whistle, soaking up the applause from delirious Welsh fans, and it summed up how far I'd travelled: from carpenter's mate to Welsh rugby history-maker.

The coaches celebrated our win, but even in victory there was a sign of how ruthless the new regime could be. Alix Popham had played for most of the game after coming on as an early replacement for JT. But, for reasons I never fathomed, he was dropped for the next match and never played for Wales again. I don't think Alix himself ever worked out why he'd had the axe, but I'm sure it's not an outcome he envisaged as he celebrated on his knees on the Twickenham turf. It was a moment of reckoning I would one day face myself.

For now though, things were on the up and up. Against Scotland the following week my confidence was sky-high. I was good under the high ball and solid in defence, chasing down winger Simon Danielli to stop a scoring opportunity. For us, Shane scored twice. By this point, I think we were all starting to sense that something special might be on the cards. If the coaches thought the same, they weren't letting on. But with a two-week break till the next match, they were happy for us to venture out into Cardiff that night. In those days, camera-phones weren't as omnipresent as they are now, and there was no controversy. We just enjoyed the evening before heading back to the Vale, ready to start work again the following Monday.

Next up was Italy, again in Cardiff. By now, I was really hitting my straps, and I scored twice at the Millennium Stadium as we put the Azzurri to the sword. Gav put me in for the first – a bit of a run-in – but the second, even if I say so myself, was pretty decent: a hand-off on Gonzalo Canale (later a good mate of mine in France) and a burst of speed to finish from the halfway line. Shane also added a third to his try tally, after which Shaun Edwards was seen yelling 'What a player!' on TV.

The game was somewhat marred for me by an incident

that happened near the end, however. I was lying at the bottom of a ruck when suddenly I felt fingers going into my eye. At the final whistle I could barely see out of it. Afterwards, I was in the changing room when the citing commissioner approached me and told me not to worry, they'd seen what had happened and had it on video. 'Are you serious?' I replied. I didn't even know what had happened myself. It turned out that Mauro Bergamasco, the Italian flanker, had gouged me – an offence for which he received an 18-week ban. Awkwardly, I found myself staying in the same hotel as Bergamasco and his girlfriend some time afterwards, whilst on holiday in Santorini with my wife Andrea. We nodded at each other over breakfast, but that's about as far as it went. Looking back, it was a pretty low thing to do.

I'd still been named Man of the Match, though, and people were starting to notice me. Warren actually said that I'd been the player of the tournament up to that point, though it was Shane who eventually claimed the title. Fair enough, I suppose. He continued to be in fantastic form, scoring again in Dublin as we edged out Ireland to claim the Triple Crown. Once again, the on-pitch celebrations at Croke Park were memorable. But, as skipper Ryan Jones lifted the Triple Crown trophy, talk was already turning to the Grand-Slam showdown with France coming up the following Saturday.

After the World Cup embarrassment it had been quite a turnaround. Understandably, much of the attention was on Gats and the coaches. What miracle had this gruff Kiwi performed, to transform the losers of Nantes into potential European champions? I've already mentioned how training had become more professional. Warren was also a master of psychology. He'd forever be telling us how good we were, saying: 'No one can live with you, no one can compete with you. You're fitter, faster and stronger than the opposition.' Then he'd claim to have the fitness stats from the Ireland or England camps, which showed that our players were indeed 5 seconds quicker or 5 kg heavier than their counterparts. Whether he really had this information, and how true it was, who knows. But the pep talks worked wonders for us mentally.

Tactically, his ideas were simple, but effective. 'Warrenball', as it's been termed, has in recent years been discredited by some, but there's no doubt it's been successful... in 2008, stratospherically so. In a nutshell, it's all about working hard to create space. First, we would attack the short side, going through the phases towards the touchline. As the space became reduced, the backs would sprint round onto the open side, giving us – in theory – a numerical advantage over the opposition, who'd been sucked into defending too narrowly.

Fine in principle. But the strategy required ceaseless work from all 15 players, both from the outside backs – who'd be forever flying from one side of the field to the other – and from the forwards who, on top of their set-piece duties, were expected to hit dozens of rucks. Luckily, we had no shortage of willing workhorses. Alun

Wyn Jones, Luke Charteris and Gethin Jenkins all had a seemingly-endless appetite for hard work. Ian Gough was another one. Nicknamed the 'professional ruck cleaner', Goughy would sometimes go an entire 80 minutes without touching the ball, but he'd hit about 30 rucks. And without that hard work, we couldn't have done what we did: you need the graft before the glory.

Everyone in the team knew his role, and was able to perform it because of all the fitness work we'd been doing under Craig White. Later, when teams started to suss out 'Warrenball', Gats told us not to worry. 'Back your fitness', he'd say, arguing that the opposition would eventually crack under the onslaught. 99% of the time (at least back then) he was right.

Work ethic was Warren's gold standard. In video sessions, he'd always praise the player who'd worked hardest off the ball, pointing out how their efforts had made a score for someone else. Very often, the guy who'd get the praise was Gavin Henson. Every week we'd analyse the GPS data from the game, showing who'd covered the most ground. Nine times out of ten it would be Gav. He'd get tackled, get up, put himself in position to receive the next pass. He may not have got the ball, but he'd be attracting a defender.

Gav was a great player. He had an unbelievable boot on him, maybe even bigger than mine (we'd have kicking contests). He had great vision, with that Regan King-like ability to put players into space with a telling pass. And he had that one quality all great players seem to possess – time. Often he'd have just milliseconds to play with, but to the onlooker it seemed like all the time in the world.

Personally, I loved his company. I used to visit him at his house in St Brides Major – complete with mirrored gym and sunbed – that he shared with his ex, Charlotte Church. More often than not, the karaoke machine would come out. Granted, he's not everyone's cup of tea, but I thought he was great for team spirit. He was different, and I like that. Strutting round in his silver boots with his tan and good looks: you need characters like that in a team. And he was a model professional when it came to looking after himself. He'd turn up to training with Tupperware boxes filled with chicken or eggs and eat the contents in his car at lunchtime. I've always prided myself on my diet, but this was next-level stuff.

Like all of us, Gav would sometimes undo the effects of his clean living with alcohol, however. We once had a pre-season trip to Loughborough with the Ospreys, and, at the end of a hard week of training, decided to have a night on the town. We were all absolutely steaming, and some of us, including Gav, were sick. The next morning, in a dehydrated state, he stepped onto the scales to be weighed by Huw Bevan, our strength and conditioning coach (a daily ritual during camp). Huw was horrified by what he saw: Gav had lost nearly 5 kg.

Huw wouldn't have been happy if he'd known about Gav's means of transportation that night, either. Six of us had wanted to travel, so we paid a taxi driver an extra £50 to take us in his five-seater: four of us in the back and Gav – who'd volunteered for the honour – in the boot. Those of a claustrophobic disposition would be horrified by this idea, but Gav seemed to enjoy it. Another time, back in Bridgend, the police stopped us on our way into town. They'd spotted six of us in the car – three in the back seat and a fourth stretched across their laps. What on earth, the officers asked, did we think we were doing? At that moment, with perfect timing, the boot popped open, revealing Gavin inside.

Some people feel Gav fell short of his potential in the game and that the pressure of being high profile from a young age got to him. But he's definitely one of the most gifted I've played with – it's crazy to think he's never played in a World Cup.

*****

Unlike 'Grand Slam day' in 2005, when Cardiff had been bathed in spring sunshine, our day of destiny was drenched by rain. Not that the weather dampened the fans' enthusiasm. Ask any player, and they'll tell you the coach trip from the Vale Resort Hotel to central Cardiff is a special experience: for me, it was never better than on 15 March 2008. Castle Street and Westgate Street were awash with red and blue despite the torrential conditions, and we received the usual wild reception from the home supporters.

In camp that week, there'd been an atmosphere of hushed expectation. We all respected how dangerous France could be, but equally, we felt quietly confident. We knew how hard we'd worked, and felt certain we had the game to break the French down. It was simply a question of executing under pressure.

In the white-hot atmosphere of the Millennium Stadium with the roof shut, that was easier said than done. But we got to work with purpose and intensity. It had been a while since we'd beaten the French on home soil, but Shane scored another of his 'specials' to put us in the box seat. Quite rightly, people remember that try, and the one scored by 'Nugget' (Martyn Williams) to seal the victory, but spare a thought for our other winger, Mark Jones. After a campaign spent in the shadow of the little genius on the opposite flank, he almost scored the try of his life in the second half. 'Boycey' got the ball on our own try line, before weaving and sprinting his way a full 80 m before being hauled down just short. It would have been a popular score with all the boys. Mark may not have enjoyed the same headlines as Shane, but was an excellent player in his own right. Always on your shoulder going forward, always working hard to get back and defend, he was a real player's player... and a full back's dream. He'd also shown bags of character to overcome the two potentially career-ending knee injuries mentioned earlier. It's a huge shame he couldn't manage that extra couple of yards.

I was pleased with my own performance, particularly in

the build-up to what proved to be our decisive try. I put an up-and-under into their 22 and chased it, rising above lock Lionel Nallet to claim the ball. Gethin smashed the ruck and, a phase or two later, Martyn threw a dummy and went in under the posts.

I had goosebumps up my arms. For me, that moment was better than the try against England. Then, I'd merely finished off the move... this time I'd made something happen. With the way we were defending (we only conceded two tries in the whole tournament) there was no way I could see France coming back into it, and they didn't. The final whistle blew, with the scoreboard reading 29-12. Wales was bouncing. We'd done it – we'd won another Grand Slam.

The celebrations lasted till the following Monday. After partying the night away in Cardiff, on the Sunday I went out with Gavin and his mates, Hooky and my mates Jon Stoker, Steve Quinn, Steve Hancock and Mark Florence in Bridgend. The day, and night, passed in a blur. After hitting the pubs in Bridgend, it was back to mine, where the festivities continued. Us three players were in the thick of it, drinking with our winners' medals around our necks. I hadn't been to bed since Friday night. My last memory is of lying in the car park of a local pub – God knows how I got home. The house was a wreck the next day, but it's much easier to wake up to a mess when you're a Grand Slam champion!

There wasn't much time to dwell on the achievement:

we had busy end to the season in store with the Ospreys. But, looking back now, that was the year I came of age as an international rugby player.

And, with a Lions tour coming up the following year, I was excited about what the future might hold.

Chapter 7

Battling the 'Boks

I've had a few injuries in my time: doing my ACL at
the Scarlets was just the start of many knee problems;
I've dislocated my thumb, broken my nose and had
ankle trouble; then there was the shoulder injury that
eventually forced me to hang up my boots altogether.
But the most painful – and certainly the most frustrating
– thing I've ever suffered from was a condition you
probably haven't heard of, and one for which there's no
cure other than rest. It's called plantar fasciitis, and it
cast a shadow over what should have been one of the
highlights of my career.

For anyone at the top end of British and Irish rugby,
the 2008/09 season was dominated by one thought – the
Lions. All those players who say in post-match interviews
that they're not thinking about it are lying. I was no
different. I'd actually missed the end-of-season tour to
South Africa following the Grand Slam due to having
keyhole surgery on the knee. But after hitting such a rich
vein of form, I was still pretty confident that, all being
well, I would be on the plane the following May. In the
Autumn of 2008, that form continued. Aptly enough the

Springboks were first up and, despite our summer defeat at their place, we felt confident on home turf. It was Andy Powell's first game for Wales and he made a huge impact with some bullocking runs. Frustratingly, we ended up losing 15-20, but I'd made a few decent breaks and felt I'd put down an early marker for that Lions jersey.

Two weeks later we faced the All Blacks, in a match remembered more for what happened before kick-off than after it. Two years previously, there'd been controversy over the haka, which New Zealand had ended up performing in their changing room following a row about the order of the anthems. Recollection of that incident, and the fact that this was Warren's first encounter against his home nation, meant the haka was a bigger-than-usual talking point for the media – and us – in the build-up.

Specifically, Gatland wanted us to think about how we were going to respond to the traditional challenge. At one point we even discussed devising our own haka (thankfully we abandoned that idea). In the end, we decided simply to face them down. No one quite knew how this would pan out, but history shows it ended up being a great piece of theatre – probably something that'll never be repeated. We faced the haka but, instead of retreating when they'd finished, stood stock still... staring them out. Not an easy thing to do against 22 pumped-up Kiwis, especially when – as in my case – you've got Ma'a Nonu staring back at you! The ref, Jonathan Kaplan, ordered our captain Ryan Jones to send us back, but he didn't. Meanwhile the crowd, who'd cottoned on to what was happening, got louder and louder. It was a Mexican standoff. Even now it makes the hairs on my arm stand up when I remember it. I was thinking, 'Bloody hell, I've never been in an atmosphere like this!' – it was that much of a cauldron. And we won the moral victory: it was the All Blacks who gave us their backs first.

Perhaps inevitably, what followed was an anticlimax. We gave New Zealand a run for their money (it was the closest we came to beating them in my time) and I thought the final score of 29-9 flattered them. But they were just too good. Once again, I saw why they were (and are) the world's number one team. No one turns defence into attack with such lightning speed. I remember getting up after making a tackle, to see them disappearing into the distance. Clinical is the word.

Not even less-ethical methods worked against the All Blacks. On the Friday before one of our encounters, we were shown a video of their 'captain's run' – that is, the supposedly closed training session conducted at the Millennium Stadium on the eve of the match. Don't ask me who captured this footage, or how – all I know is that a video popped up on our laptops that evening. It's probably fair to say most unions have indulged in similar skulduggery. We always assumed WE were being secretly filmed when playing abroad. For that reason we'd never have a full training session at the venue where the game would be played, opting instead just to send the kickers out to get used to conditions. Which is exactly what the Kiwis did back in Cardiff – meaning our footage was useless. It could have been worse: Sitiveni Sivivatu once told me how New Zealand would sometimes deliberately rehearse a set of dummy moves, just to confuse prying eyes. Another example, I suppose, of the cleverness that makes them the leading team in world rugby.

So, another defeat. But there was still one more match to come, against another side who've tended to have the better of us: Australia. But on this occasion we were playing at our peak and determined not to finish the series without a major scalp.

The match started with one of the biggest collisions I've ever seen, between Jamie Roberts and Stirling Mortlock. Mortlock, their captain, was taken off there and then. Jamie, who suffered a fractured skull, followed before the end of the half, but not before he'd helped set up our first try, finished in the corner by Shane. We played some great rugby in that match. Looking back, that was when 'Warrenball' was at its most effective. All the fitness work we'd been doing under Craig White was starting to pay dividends, our defence under Shaun was rock solid, and we were able to deploy Gatland's tactics of exhausting the short side before using the full width of the pitch. This strategy was still new at international level then, and sides were struggling to live with it.

Gats and the coaches put a premium on what they called 'ball in play' time. Warren had studied footage of New Zealand and worked out that they kept the ball alive for an average of 32 minutes. Before his arrival, our average had been 25 minutes – he wanted us to improve our stats. In each match, a target would be set for 'ball in play' time. If we didn't fulfil it, we'd have to do a fitness session later to make up the difference. In that Australia game we kept the ball in play for 35 minutes – a record for us at that stage. Our confidence was sky high: at one point in that game I fielded a Wallaby kick behind our try line. Instead of dabbing it down for the dropout, I just smashed it back into Aussie territory – we backed our defence to take anything they threw at us.

The Wallabies did snatch a try back, thanks to an interception from their second row Mark Chisholm, but by now we were playing really well. Again we stretched them wide, first one way then the other, before Martyn took the ball up the middle. Back it came, Shane went on a diagonal run and popped it up for me, and then it was just like mathematics. I've since been told that dyslexic people tend to have superior spatial awareness – in sporting terms, the ability to see a gap – and the phenomenon certainly showed itself on that occasion. There was an eerie silence as I went through under the posts. On the video you can see me looking back towards the referee – I was wondering if he was going to pull me back for an infringement – but the try was good.

That win – 21-18 – was a career highlight and, to date, the last time that we beat Australia. It was also around this time that Jeremy Guscott – the ex-England and Lions centre turned media pundit – said in the press that I was playing as well as anyone in the world. It was nice of him to say it, but I can honestly say I hadn't thought about that. Most pundits seemed to have me down for the Lions tour, so I suppose that meant I was one of the form full backs in Britain and Ireland. But being dubbed the world's best... that's not a tagline I felt comfortable with.

In fact, unlike my former teammate and good friend Mike Phillips (who once asked why his plane ticket said 'club class' instead of 'world class'), praise is not something that sits well with me. It's one thing when it's in the media, but whenever family or friends told me I'd played well, I'd try and change the subject. Tell Mike he's the best player in the world and he'll say, 'You don't need to tell me – I know!' – whereas I'd get embarrassed. Perhaps it shows I'm not as confident as I should be. Perhaps it goes back to my unusual path to the top flight – who knows. Sometimes I do wish I had a bit more cockiness about me, though: I might have enjoyed my career and achievements more. Then again, perhaps I wouldn't have put in the work in the first place.

Whether we had a world-beating full back or not, Wales were defending Six Nations champions and, rightly, favourites going into the 2009 tournament. As it turned out, we actually finished fourth, although that was a slightly harsh outcome considering we only lost two games, and those by narrow margins. We'd managed to see off Scotland and England but came unstuck against France in Paris (despite me scoring one of my favourite tries, again hitting a good angle to completely flummox the French defence), then narrowly saw off Italy to set up a Championship decider against Ireland in Cardiff. A win by 13 points or more would see us claim the Six Nations crown for a second consecutive year, whereas victory for our visitors would give them their first Grand Slam since 1948. A big game, then.

In the build-up, Warren put up a list of 'possibles' and 'probables' for the Lions tour in the team room. I, together with the likes of Shane, Gethin, and Mike, was in the 'probables' column. Others, like Mark Jones, were in the 'possibles'. A good performance could make all the difference. Of course, as it turned out, it was Ireland who won the day – you'll remember Stephen Jones' last-gasp penalty dipping agonisingly short of the posts. Defeat not only doomed us to a fourth-place finish – which also meant less bonus money – but presumably also put a terminal dent in some individuals' Lions prospects. But I had my own reasons for feeling gloomy as I watched the wild Irish celebrations unfold on the Millennium Stadium turf: I'd had to go off after half an hour, nursing a mysterious and painful foot injury which, I feared, might keep me off the plane to South Africa altogether.

Plantar Fasciitis is a condition afflicting the plantar fascia – in layman's terms, the connective tissue on the bottom of the foot between the heel and toes. It occurs when this area becomes damaged or torn. In my case, the onset of this condition was something I became instantly aware of as I was sprinting along the touchline: a sudden, audible snap and flash of pain in my foot, with the result that I could barely stand on it, let alone run.

I was taken off and later given the diagnosis. I was told surgery wasn't an option: it was simply a case of resting it and letting the healing process take its course.

With just a month till the squad was named, it was a frustrating time. By day I'd head to the 'barn' (the WRU indoor training centre at the Vale of Glamorgan, which Wales uses as its training HQ), where I'd work out with Craig White, doing altitude training to simulate the South African high veldt. At night I'd have to sleep in a special sock designed to keep my toes straight. Getting up to use the loo was torture – I'd keep a golf ball at my bedside to 'warm up' the foot before hobbling to the bathroom. One comfort in all this was that I felt I'd already done enough to book my place on the plane to South Africa. It wasn't as if a few more games for the Ospreys were going to make any difference in the selectors' minds.

As it was, the worst of the foot problem had passed when the time came for the touring party to be announced. It was the first occasion the announcement had been made live on Sky Sports, so the Ospreys coaches arranged for us to take a break from training (underway, for some reason, at 'the barn') so we could watch. I don't mean to sound arrogant when I say that it didn't come as a great surprise to hear my name read out. As with my World Cup rejection two years before, it hadn't been hard to see the writing on the wall. For all the joy in the camp, though (a then record six Ospreys got the nod), there was heartbreak for others. Ryan Jones, the Wales captain, and Hooky were high-profile casualties.

It was tough to know what to say to them afterwards. There was lots of handshaking, congratulations to some and commiserations to others. Training resumed that afternoon – which, with hindsight, was a mistake. It would have been better to send everyone home.

For the lucky ones who'd had the nod, though, there was little time to get used to our new status as Lions. There were suits to be fitted for, image rights to be signed away, contracts to be digested. The squad gathered at Pennyhill Park, normally England's base. The first day was given over to media interviews and general mingling. At 8 p.m. we were in our rooms (I was sharing with Joe Worsley) when the phone rang with the message: 'Meet in the bar straight away.' The coaches were waiting for us, brandishing boxes of fancy dress. Each player had to select an item. My roommate Mr Worsley was, as it turned out, a more-than-useful pianist, and he led the singing, along with guitar strummers like Andrew Sheridan. The revelries lasted long into the night. It was a great bit of team bonding, although, believe it or not, I'd actually been hoping for a dry start to the tour!

The familiarity of training made our hangovers easier to bear. With Gats, Shaun and Rob all in the coaching line-up, many of the routines were those we were already used to with Wales. These included the so-called 'minute drill', which involved three attackers and six defenders, all in full body armour, going at each other for 60 seconds. It was a routine that claimed a few injury victims on that tour, starting with the unfortunate Irishman Jerry

Flannery, who was ruled out before we even left home soil. Naturally, the Welsh boys started at an advantage when it came to these drills, though it didn't take the likes of Brian O'Driscoll long to get the hang of them.

*****

My big rival for a test shirt was Ireland's Rob Kearney, but I was handed the first opportunity to impress, in the tour opener against the Royal XV. The playing squad headed upcountry for the match at Rustenburg, a small city in the countryside of North West Province. We stayed in wooden lodges and had to keep the shutters closed for fear of the monkeys looting our possessions. It was also the first time I'd had to contend with mosquitoes during a game – some as big as your hand. But it was the Royal XV – a scratch side made up mostly of amateurs – who turned out to be the biggest threats to our well-being. With a chunk of the second half gone, and our hosts leading 25-13, a major upset was on the cards. After all, the last time the Lions had lost a tour opener was in 1971. At this point I took a pass from Shane and launched a speculative up-and-under from inside our half. I managed to get a boot to it when it landed and another when it bounced the second time, before gathering to score. It's probably my favourite try ever, even better than the one in Paris earlier that season, and it started a comeback. Another couple of scores and we'd nicked it – not that it saved us from a bollocking from the coaches afterwards.

We started to find our feet after that, though, stringing together some impressive wins over the Super 14 teams. Off the field, meanwhile, I was enjoying getting to know players from the other nations. Most days on the bus I'd sit next to Euan Murray, the Scottish tight-head. Apparently Euan had been a bit of a wild character in his young days, but all that changed after he'd been knocked unconscious during a game: afterwards, he became a born-again Christian. Euan would talk to me about God as we travelled to training. Later, when he returned home due to injury, he gave me a copy of the Bible, with a nice message inside, which I've still got. Despite my Catholic upbringing, I don't think there's much chance of me being 'born again', but it was a kind gesture.

Then there was Riki Flutey, the English centre and another of the tour musicians. We appreciated his guitar skills at squad social events, but it was still a surprise to see him strumming away on a rest day at a Cape Town shopping mall, guitar case open for donations. Perhaps I should have tipped him more generously, as it was around the time that I'd boosted my tour earnings thanks to some sage betting advice from one Ronan O'Gara, with whom I'd been rooming. One afternoon, 'Rog' informed me that he'd had a tip from a friend back in Ireland, and that I'd be well advised to 'get on' this particular horse. It was good advice indeed: I staked a grand at 5-1, thus ending up £4,000 to the good... though the win did start a gambling habit which didn't always end so lucratively.

Ronan and I were involved in another, rather sad

incident during our time in Cape Town. We'd just returned from a session of 'sea recovery' in the Atlantic (very, very cold). Every time we went out as a squad we had security with us, as you have to be careful in South Africa. But when we got back to the hotel room, we found a small boy in our bathroom. How he'd got in, we weren't exactly sure. A favourite technique for robbers was to pose as cleaning staff and tactically drop a towel on the floor as you were leaving, thus preventing the door from closing properly. This kid hadn't nicked any of the posh electronic gear we'd left in the room, though: instead, his pockets were full of soap and toiletries. It was sad to see. We just let him go and didn't mention it to security.

In Johannesburg, you had to be particularly careful. We were staying at a hotel in Sandton City, and had hired some ex-special forces guys to stand guard outside. We'd been given strict instructions not to leave the complex. But temptation was ever-present. The hotel was a stopover for airline staff passing through, and there was an arrivals board in the foyer. When a plane was due in, all the single guys would splash on the aftershave and head downstairs to the bar, to greet the female cabin crew as they arrived (this was before I met Andrea!).

It was all good fun, but I nearly came to regret leaving the safety of the hotel one night. This girl I'd met suggested she come and pick me up so we could go on a date. I managed to sneak past the SBS boys outside the hotel and jump in her car, and we headed off to a quiet spot to chat. Before long, though, I noticed this van circling us, containing about six not very friendly-looking guys. Jo'burg has one of the highest murder rates in the world, and I didn't fancy adding to the statistics. I asked the girl to take me back to the hotel, whilst resolving to heed the safety advice in future.

We will still managed to do a fair bit of socialising in other parts of the country, though, and skipper Paul O'Connell was as up for it as anyone. Paul was great as a captain and as a bloke. His inspirational leadership is well documented, but he also enjoys 'the craic', as the Irish would put it. One evening in his company stands out. We were in a club where they had a spinning-wheel on the bar: each spin would see the wheel land on a different alcohol shot which would then have to be consumed – a sort of boozy roulette. Paul and I got the hang of it pretty quickly. 'Again, Byrney, again! Spin the wheel, Byrney!' he kept saying. So spin it again I did. Who was I to disobey orders from the Lions captain?!

*****

The wheel of fortune had certainly been turning my way on tour. I'd scored another try against the Natal Sharks – Brian O'Driscoll floated a pass out and I stepped inside my old Ospreys colleague Stefan Terblanche on my way to the try line. I was playing as well as I could remember. Much had been made of my supposed rivalry with Kearney, but I was doing my talking out on the pitch, and was deservedly in pole position for the first test against the Springboks in Durban. We knew we were in for a tough task – up against the world champions in their own backyard – but we'd started playing some good stuff and were quietly confident about our chances.

I can't describe how exciting the build-up to the game was. My family had arrived the week before, and Durban was a sea of red. Willie John McBride handed out the test jerseys. I was feeling tip-top as I ran out at the ABSA stadium for the pre-match warm up in front of a packed and vocal crowd.

And then it happened.

The sensation was exactly the same as the one I'd experienced during the Ireland match – a sudden, sharp pain and snapping sound at the base of my foot. I immediately called the physio over, whilst trying to play down what had happened in front of the watching cameras. I was helped to the changing room where I told him to strap it up – then I continued to hit the tackle bags indoors. At this point the adrenalin was coursing through my veins, masking the pain: pulling out wasn't an option. Mentally though, I was already compromised. As I ran out onto the pitch and stood for the anthems, the confidence I'd experienced beforehand evaporated; my head was filled with nagging doubts about my foot and how it would affect me. Perhaps I hoped I'd be able to run it off. I soon realised that wasn't going to happen. I made a half-break early on, but the pain was getting worse and I wasn't able to run properly. With 37 minutes on the clock (and us trailing badly after a poor start) I bowed to the inevitable, and came off.

It was one of the most gutting feelings I've ever had. I'd gone from feeling on top of the world to crocked, with my tour in serious doubt, and to top it all we'd lost the test, despite a second-half comeback. I was assessed afterwards and Geech (Ian McGeechan) told me he wanted me to stay in South Africa and sit on the bench for the second game, now a must-win if we wanted to keep the series alive. My foot was far from right, but I'd been handed a tiny sliver of hope. But then, in training, I dislocated my thumb following a collision with Keith Earls. That was that – curtains for my Lions tour.

It was hugely disappointing. I got a good send-off from South Africa, going out for ten pints with the other Fab Four members (Hooky had by now joined the touring party), but naturally I wondered what might have been. I was luckier than many, and I can always say I won a Lions cap. But the experience had been tainted by the injury. It wouldn't have been so bad if it had happened during the game; at least I'd have been able to enjoy the excitement of running out onto the pitch and all the rest of it. But to go out knowing I was crocked before we'd even kicked off overshadowed the moment.

I was only able to watch on TV as the rest of the series unfolded. We lost an epic second test (still remembered as one of the most physical games ever) and with it the series, though our consolation victory in Johannesburg – together with the general way we'd acquitted ourselves on tour – was thought at the time to have done much to restore the credibility of the Lions brand.

I'd still say that being a Lion, and travelling to South Africa (it turned out to be my only rugby trip there) was a great time in my life. It's a beautiful and diverse country, though obviously one that still has its share of social problems. Visiting the townships, meeting the kids who seem so happy – despite having so little – was humbling. And of course I treasure the rugby experiences and the friendships I made. It's said that there's a special bond between Lions, something that stays with you no matter how long it's been since you last saw each other, and I'd say that's true.

And despite the disappointing way my tour had ended, it had been another great year for me personally. My stock had never been higher, thanks in no small part to a certain Mr Guscott, who'd made those complimentary comments about me the previous autumn. Not long afterwards, I bumped into Jerry at an event in London, bought him a Jägerbomb, and thanked him for adding a few zeros onto my next contract. We laughed, but I meant every word. You can't put a price on publicity like that. Was I the best full back in the world in 2009? I'll leave that to the rugby historians to judge. But it certainly felt like it for a while... and part of the credit for that must go to my English friend. Cheers, Jerry!

At a family wedding with Mum, Dad and my sister Siân

In the back garden with Siân and Dusty, our dog

Family shot

St Mary's RC Primary School rugby team, with Mr Steele. I'm just behind the boy with the ball.

Tie presentation for West Wales Under 11s – I'm in the middle at the back

A Lion in the making – with my mum, aged about 10

On holiday in Cala d'Or, Mallorca in about 1996, aged 16 – Rhys Florence, Carle Ellis, me and a random!

Aged 17, having a few cans in the garden with my friend Carl Tozer

Playing for Bridgend Athletic

Tondu team line-up – I'm at the front, 2nd from left

Getting tackled by Aled Thomas – Scarlets v. Dragons

Fending off Anthony Elliott – Scarlets v. Newcastle

England v. Wales in 2008 – the famous try!

Mystery guest on *A Question of Sport*, with Jerry Rice

Calling a mark in the first Test against South Africa on the 2009 Lions tour

Me, Jerry and my mate Jon Stoker

Going past Jamie Heaslip on the way to the tryline in the 2010 Magners Grand Final at the RDS

Celebrating the Ospreys' Grand Final win

With my cousins
Jessica and
Kimberly and
Aunty Hazel

Making a break
v. Italy in the Six
Nations

The Fab Four on
tour – the 2011
World Cup in
New Zealand

My last night out on a Wales tour – Brewy, Hooky, Shane, Phillsy and me

Clermont pre-season army camp, with Noa Nakataki and Regan King

My mates from Wales visiting me at Clermont

Warming up for Clermont

My best moment as Dragons
captain, winning in Paris
against Stade Français

Andrea and me at our wedding on the Glanusk Estate, 2012

JC and me on my wedding day

JC, Nikki Walker and me at my wedding

With Andrea on holiday in Budapest

Andrea and me at Alex Lapandry and Rachel Goodman's house in Clermont Auvergne

With Alex Lapandry and Mike Delaney

With Mark Florence and Gerald McCarthy, mates from Bridgend

Holiday in Marbella, 2014.
L–R: Mark Florence, Carle Ellis, Dan Williams, Rhys Webb and Chris Harris

With Brendan Roach, my mentor growing up

With Jonah Lomu and Sonny Bill Williams at Jerry's house the night before the funeral. Jonah died just a few months later.

Outside the venue for Jerry's funeral with the whole gang

With the children at Tomorrow's Generation

After retirement – before Wales v. South Africa at the 2015 World Cup, Twickenham

With my Uncle Andrew

Out on the Mumbles: L–R: Shane, Phillsy, Brewy, Tash, Hooky, Bish and Alan Wyn

With Chris Masoe and Dan Carter

With my family at my sister Siân's wedding

Andrea and me with my cousin Julian and his wife Zoe in NZ

Meeting the Earl of Wessex at the Duke of Edinburgh Awards

With Mum at the Duke of Edinburgh Awards

CHAPTER 8

High Times

I'm sure there were more unpopular blokes in Scotland than me in 2011 (they're still not big fans of King Edward II, even 700 years on), but I reckon I'd have been up there. By the end of that year's Six Nations, I'd personally brought the international careers of two of their players to an end, had been shown a yellow card for high tackling another, and was still being blamed for what (depending on your point of view) was either the biggest surrender, or the biggest comeback, in Six Nations history.

Of course, I take no pleasure in the career-ending bits. In the case of Thom Evans, I'm eternally grateful it wasn't worse. Thom, you'll remember, damaged his neck in an incident involving me at the Millennium Stadium in 2010. As often seems the case with near-catastrophic injuries, it had looked innocuous enough. I'd gone to tackle him, but Shane got there first. As Thom fell, his head connected with my groin area, and snapped backwards. It was lucky the arriving players rucked over him as he lay: we learned later that he'd have been paralysed – at best – if anyone had landed on top of him.

He still needed emergency surgery in Cardiff that night,

followed by another operation the week after. Apparently his vertebrae had been knocked so badly out of kilter that he'd been just a millimetre from never walking again... or worse. It was a sobering moment for me, to think that I'd been involved – albeit unintentionally – in an incident that nearly cost someone his life. I texted Thom to say sorry. A few years later, we made contact and went out for a drink. Since then, we've become quite good mates. I still apologise to him sometimes for what happened (normally after we've had few beers), but I think he's forgiven me. Given how his modelling and acting career has taken off since his retirement, you could say I did him a favour!

That said, I'm sure the Scots thought I had it in for the Evans clan the following year, when I was sin-binned for high tackling his brother Max. That was also the game where Hugo Southwell needed 40+ stitches after I caught him in the face with my studs (I was airborne at the time). Hugo never played for Scotland again. Then there was the Geoff Cross incident of 2009, where the prop was yellow carded AND stretchered off with a knee injury after taking me out in the air. You can see why I was considered a jinx north of the border.

But back to that Cardiff encounter of 2010 which – the Thom Evans scare apart – is remembered as one of the great escape acts in Welsh rugby history. It had been a strangely lethargic performance on our part, and, with the scoreboard reading 24-14 to Scotland with 14 minutes left, we looked dead and buried. Then Scott Lawson was shown a yellow card, and gaps started to appear. Shane wove some magic and put me into space, and I was able to draw my man and put Halfpenny in to score. From the kick-off we went straight back on the attack. Jamie Roberts made a half-break and put me into a hole, but I could see the cover coming across and kicked ahead. As I sprinted through, I felt contact and went down... the video shows that Phil Godman – just back on following a head injury and swathed in bandages – had tripped me. Afterwards Andy Robinson, the Scotland coach, accused me of diving. I may have made a meal of it, but I definitely felt contact. In any event, Godman was off, Scotland were down to 13, and Stephen Jones kicked a penalty to make it all square: 24-24.

The Scots should have kicked it dead from the restart and taken the draw – they were out on their feet. But for some reason, they gave it back to us and... you know what happened next. Looking back, I was lucky to get away with a forward pass in the build-up to the winning try – the ball which put Halfpenny away down the right looks a bit more than perpendicular on the video. But the flag stayed down, we recycled, and Shane went over, to scenes of pandemonium. I wasn't bothered when I heard about Robinson's accusation afterwards. Like everyone else, he probably couldn't believe that Scotland had lost – we barely could ourselves.

The coaches – no doubt as relieved as we were – gave us the green light to go out in Cardiff that night. The celebrations which followed have become almost as famous as the win itself. The evening began in Walkabout

Bar on Cardiff's St Mary Street. There was a cordoned-
off area for the team and their friends, and pretty soon
everyone was leathered. Powelly had his top off – it was
mayhem. I was as drunk as I've ever been, and had to
be carried out before being kindly transported back to
the Vale Hotel in a police car. By the time I got there, I'd
gathered enough of a second wind to join Shane, Powelly,
JT and a few others at the bar. There was no way we
wanted this party to stop.

2 a.m. rolled round and with it, closing time; Andy was
trying, and failing, to get room service so we could carry
on drinking. As we stumbled through the doors at the
front of the hotel, he started messing about with one of
the golf buggies parked outside. The rest of us were doing
the same – I dimly remember hanging onto the back of
Powelly's buggy before falling off. My last memory was of
seeing the big man driving off into the distance. My race
was run, and I turned in.

The next morning, feeling none too grand, I turned
on Sky Sports News and discovered what had happened
next: Andy had been arrested after driving the golf
buggy down the M4 motorway. He'd actually made it to
the service station at the next junction, where he told
police he'd been going to buy a sandwich and some
fags. Despite his inebriated condition, he'd apparently
had the foresight to put a flashing traffic cone on the
roof in a doomed effort to make the buggy roadworthy.
I tried phoning him but couldn't get through (it turned
out he'd been otherwise engaged at the police station).

After several failed attempts, I eventually made contact at 11 o'clock that evening. Andy spoke first: 'You were fucking hammered last night, weren't you?' he said. 'Powelly – have you turned on the TV? You're all over the news!' There was a pause: 'Yeah. Good night though, wasn't it?'

The festivities cost Powelly his driving licence as well as his place in the Six Nations squad. But he wasn't the only one to suffer the consequences of our big night out. A few days later, I was doing some video analysis in the team room when I felt a tap on my shoulder. It was Alan Phillips, the team manager. 'What's this then, son?' he said, in that characteristic way of his, while waving a sheet of paper under my nose. 'What's what?' I replied. He showed me the paper. It was a printout of an e-mail he'd had earlier that day. I read it: it was from the mother of a young lady who claimed to have met me in Walkabout on the Saturday night.

Now, at the time, I'd been wearing a rather expensive-looking Hublot watch. I say 'expensive-looking' because it was actually fake: bought on a trip to Dubai earlier that season. It was a good copy, mind – it looked the bollocks – but somewhere along the way during the post-match celebrations I'd managed to lose it. I'd thought no more about it, but, reading the e-mail, it turned out I'd given the watch to this girl, who checked it out online and thought she'd hit the jackpot. She apparently told her mother she was going to sell it and use the money to pay her college fees, only to be left disappointed when she got to the pawn shop and discovered its true value... about £10, not £10,000.

I didn't see what I'd done wrong in the whole episode, but Alan insisted on inviting mother and daughter to the Vale so I could have lunch with them, by way of apology. This was a common sight when we were in camp – a sheepish-looking player sitting awkwardly at the table with some members of the public – and to the trained eye could mean only one thing: the player had fucked up the weekend before. It became a running joke – you could always tell who'd been a naughty boy if they were sitting at the table on Monday lunchtime. Personally, I thought the offended parties in my case had a bit of a nerve. After all, the girl had taken my watch, tried to sell it, and then had the gall to write in complaining that it wasn't real! I didn't even get it back, either.

The whole tactic of inviting people to the hotel was largely intended to keep incidents out of the paper. Sadly, sometimes the damage had already been done. In 2009, we beat England at the Millennium Stadium to make it two from two in that year's Six Nations. We'd played well, and since there was no game the following week, the management gave us licence to go out and enjoy ourselves. So the Sunday following the game saw Phillsy, Henson, Powelly, JT, Rhys Thomas and I head out for a few beers. After a couple at the Three Golden Cups in Bridgend, we caught taxis into Cardiff, where we carried on the session at the Queen's Vaults pub opposite the

Millennium Stadium. As the beers flowed, things got a bit heated. Gav kicked a barstool from under JT, who'd fallen asleep. JT retaliated by shoving Gav, who in turn hurled a pool ball across the bar, smashing one of the optics.

At this point, we thought it best to leave. We beat a hasty retreat onto St Mary Street – only to be collared by the police, who'd been informed of the trouble. Powelly started getting agitated so they put him in the back of the van to calm down, but for the most part they were remarkably good about it. They even ordered a bystander who was filming the incident on his mobile to delete the footage. By now, Powelly was shaking the van back and forth like a caged gorilla. Henson, also the worse for wear, was trying to smooth things over by flicking banknotes at the policemen in a jokey bid to 'buy us out.' Luckily for us, they had a sense of humour about it all. So, while the pub flare-up made the papers, none of the other stuff did.

Everyone's got a video camera in their pocket these days, that's the trouble. I'm not saying we always cover ourselves in glory on the piss, mind, and there are one or two who always seem to attract trouble. Phillsy, for one, although he'd tell you that's because he's an easy target! He's my mate of course, so I always keep an eye out for him on nights out (provided I'm in any fit state myself). In the latter years of my career, we started avoiding Cardiff altogether, preferring to go out in Bridgend for a few pints and a bit of karaoke. You couldn't guarantee avoiding hassle there either, but it was less likely.

Since I'm on the subject of Sunday sessions, there's another one I should tell you about, which also almost ended with an unwelcome appearance in the newspapers. Sunday was a big drinking day if there was no training on the Monday. This one time, I went out in Porth in the Rhondda with Andrew Bishop and his brother David. We started in the rugby club at midday before going on a pub crawl. At the end of the night, bladdered, I got a taxi back to Bridgend. Unfortunately, I spewed inside the cab. Then, to add insult to injury, I discovered I'd lost my bank card so was unable to pay the driver for the cleaning costs. He was less than amused, and left me stranded on some street in the middle of nowhere in the freezing cold. I started knocking on doors – thankfully some kind stranger took me in, and I crashed on their sofa.

The next morning, I woke up wondering where the fuck I was, and eventually made my way home. But back in camp that week, I was taken aside by our Head of Communications John Williams. He told me that the disgruntled taxi driver was threatening to take his story to the *News of the World*... unless I paid him a couple of grand. To make matters worse, the cabbie had video evidence of me being sick in his car. This was extortion, pure and simple. Luckily, a friend put me in touch with a couple of local heavies in the area. They paid the driver a visit, gave him the money I owed, and persuaded him to not push his luck any further. No story appeared in the *News of The World*, but it was another narrow escape.

My liking for a weekend bender didn't always go

unpunished, however. In November 2010, I fractured my thumb playing for Wales against New Zealand in Cardiff. I knew it was bad straight away, and told the physio, Hywel Griffiths, that I wanted to come off. The message came down that I was to stay on, however – and I proceeded to have a nightmare, despite scoring a consolation try. Afterwards I was gutted, and drowned my sorrows with drink. As a result, I missed a consultation with the specialist arranged for the Monday morning. By the time the problem was diagnosed, I'd gone nearly a week without treatment, meaning a longer layoff. The Ospreys were less than pleased, and put out a press statement which left the reader in no doubt about where they thought the blame lay.

*****

This was around the time my star was at its highest, and no shortage of money-making opportunities came my way. There were some great sponsorship deals – Guinness, Jaguar and Maximuscle to name but three. The Jaguar deal meant I got to drive around in some top-of-the-range cars, which was great, but again also landed me in a spot of bother.

I'd been driving up to London one day in my V6 F-type sport, a beast of a car that could really shift. It took me about an hour and a half to get there from Bridgend. Unbeknown to me, an unmarked police car was in pursuit, but I was going so fast it gave up the chase. I was later informed that I'd been doing 145 mph. 100 mph is an instant ban: 145, for all I knew, could have meant a jail sentence. I was summonsed to appear in court in Swindon. Luckily, I was able to enlist the help of my neighbour, solicitor Dan Williams. Dan – known affectionately by his friends as 'Mr Loophole' – successfully challenged the measurement made by the police camera. As a result, we got the speed revised down to 100mph. I was still banned from driving for 56 days and hit with a £4,500 fine, but it could have been a whole lot worse. And, although I had to take taxis everywhere for the next two months, we again managed to keep the story out of the papers.

A newspaper scandal wouldn't have done much for my marketability. I certainly wouldn't have ended up doing my Cash for Gold TV adverts, which proved particularly lucrative. I made a few ads for the company – one on a rugby pitch, one where I was jumping into a pool – and whilst I'm unlikely to make the shortlist for the next Oscars, I was certainly well paid for my trouble.

I should also thank Cash for Gold for introducing me to the attention of my lovely wife, Andrea. The ads would come on each evening just before the ITV Wales News (where she works as one of the main presenters), and she'd be in the studio watching – and no doubt having a good laugh – with the rest of the crew. Not long afterwards we made contact (I messaged her on Twitter) and we met up, and the rest is history. So, by all means:

go ahead and say my acting's wooden – I wouldn't have missed Cash for Gold for the world!

Some of my other forays onto the small screen were less well advised, however. Like the time I appeared on the Channel 5 show 'Sex: How to Do Everything', which is still occasionally repeated now. The brief was to appear as part of a panel and talk about... sex. With me, the angle was how sex affects sporting performance, and whether I personally would abstain, or indulge, before a big game. For some reason, and I still don't know why I said this, I told them I would always relieve myself – solo – before the match to ease my nerves. This isn't actually true, honest! But the odd person still reminds me about my ill-judged remark.

While we're on the subject of sex, perhaps now would be a good time to lay one myth to rest – that I am gay. The rumour started around the time that I left the Scarlets for the Ospreys, and whilst I have no proof of this, I wouldn't be surprised if it was started by a disgruntled fan in the Llanelli area. It wouldn't be the first time, of course, that there's been speculation about a rugby player's sexuality. Nine times out of ten, though, it's all bollocks. In my case, it was put about that I was seeing Nigel Owens, the referee. Nigel, a successful comic as well as a ref, was at pains to deny this, announcing during after dinner speeches, 'I can confirm I am not in a relationship with Lee Byrne,' but the rumours persisted. During my single days, girls I was chatting up would sometimes say, 'It's such a shame you're gay.'

Men have also approached me via social media, offering me thousands of pounds in return for a 'discreet' hotel meet-up (although I suspect some of these 'admirers' may actually be tabloid newspaper reporters looking for a sting). So, just to put the record straight, so to speak: whilst I am certainly not homophobic, and have no objection to being a gay pin-up (if that's what I am), you wouldn't be my type, guys – even if I wasn't happily married to my gorgeous wife.

I will put my hand up to being a bit cavalier with my cash, however. I've spent a lot and, in common with other sportsmen, lost my fair share through gambling, too. For me personally, the habit started on the Lions tour, as I mentioned earlier. But there was no shortage of kindred spirits in the Wales camp – coaches and players alike. It ended up becoming a bit of an obsession for us: we'd do lots of 'spot betting' – that is, gambling on who'd win the next point in a given sporting contest. Often the sport would be really obscure: German handball or Chinese table tennis, or a beach-volleyball match between Brazil and Italy. It was utter madness, really. Like all gamblers, I had some great successes – like the time I won several thousand on a football spread bet – but some equally sobering losses. A particular stinger was the time I put £15,000 on Andy Murray, at 1-15, to beat John Isner in a first-round match in some ATP tournament. Murray lost.

Unsurprisingly, I won most often on rugby. I never bet on a game I was playing in (it's against the rules) but my insider knowledge would come in handy when putting a bet on, say, Glasgow v. Ulster in the Pro12. I was cleaning up most weeks, to the point where the manager at my local bookies eventually banned me from gambling on the game altogether.

Other big wins were down entirely to chance. One time, I was at the roulette table at a casino in Cardiff Bay. I was injured and on crutches. I put a £2,000 on black – it won; I did the same with £4,000, then £8,000; same outcome. Adrenalin flowing, I bet on black again. As the wheel slowed, it looked for all the world like it was going to finish on red. Disgusted, I left the table. But then I heard a cry behind me – I hobbled back to find the wheel had again landed on black. This time, I wasn't about to push my luck. I fought off the other players, who were trying to get their hands on my chips, and had the staff scoop them into cartons. I left the casino much better off than I'd gone in.

But of course a gambler only ever tells you what he's won, never what he's lost. For me, a turning point came when Andrea moved in and unwittingly opened one of my bank statements. We hadn't been together all that long, and she was shocked to read I'd done a couple of thousand in a month (small beer, it must be said, compared with some of my losses). She gave me what for, and I had to acknowledge that things had got out of hand. Happily, I haven't had a bet since. I feel lucky that I've been able to quit so easily – others have found it much harder. I suppose it's a strength of mine: although I'd say I have an addictive personality, when I DO decide to quit something, I can do it more less straight away. In this case, I'd certainly needed a push in the right direction from Andrea, mind you. It took me a while to realise it, but she's definitely changed my life for the better. Perhaps, if I hadn't met her, I'd still be gambling today.

CHAPTER 9

World Cup woes

When you've been in any team for a while, you get used
to hearing your name read out in the starting XV. It's not
that you take your place for granted, it's just you grow
to expect it – and when the day dawns that it doesn't
happen, it comes as a big shock. That's what happened
to me in the final week of September 2011. I was in
New Zealand. It was the World Cup – rugby's biggest
showpiece – and the opposition was Samoa in a must-win
pool game. As usual, Gats started with the full back: 'Full
back: Leigh... Halfpenny.' It took a second to compute:
Halfpenny, not Byrne. This wasn't a meaningless match,
but one we had to win to progress to the last eight. I
wasn't even on the bench. I didn't know where to look: it
was a big turning point in my career.

Looking back, the problems had started earlier that
summer. My knee, by now subject to many years of
wear and tear, was wrecked. I'd had another operation
at the end of the season, after which my surgeon, David
Pemberton, had made a grim prognosis: 'It's bone to
bone. There's no cartilage left. You may have to pack
it in.' I'd known things were bad. My running gait had

changed, my pace was down. I was no longer able to get full flexibility in the joint. Now I'd more or less been told that I was in the last-chance saloon.

I soon began to notice the effects on my performance. Adam Beard, by now the Wales fitness coach, had the team in for testing before we set off for our pre-tournament training camp in Poland. He had us doing Watt tests, which involve lots of sprinting. I'd always prided myself on my conditioning, but for the first time in my career I found myself being blitzed by my teammates. My knee just wasn't allowing me to perform at the required level.

It was the same story out in Spala, where we headed for our training camp that summer. I was forced to watch from under a pitch-side marquee as the boys were put through drill after gruelling drill, a passive onlooker as they became fitter, faster and stronger. Meanwhile, I lay there being pummelled by our masseur – a Polish guy by the name of Lukasz Kuzmicki. Lukasz was trying to get my leg to straighten: he'd be leaning on the joint with his full body weight, striving in vain to get it to the horizontal. By day it was physio and rehab; by night, I'd slink off to the gym to use the leg press in an effort to get the knee working, but it was desperately slow progress.

By the second week, I was starting to notice some small improvement. Adam had us doing a drill called 'runways', where you start off flat on your stomach before sprinting to a cone then repeating the process. It was

pissing down with rain, but funnily enough I killed it –
although maybe that's because I was fresh and the others
were knackered from all the training. I couldn't believe it:
at the time I could barely walk properly, let alone run. But
despite that performance, I was still far from right. My
kicking – always one of my main weapons – was suffering
particularly badly. I recall Jenks shouting encouragement
to me during practice, but, try as I might, I just couldn't
do it.

When we got back from Spala I had a week's holiday
on the Greek island of Santorini with Andrea. I hoped
the sun and rest would do the knee some good, but I
was wrong. I could hear it crunching whenever I walked
upstairs. It certainly didn't help the holiday mood – I was
stressed out and we argued. By now I was beginning to
realise the seriousness of my situation, and even talked
with Andrea about the possibility of quitting altogether. I
still wasn't right when I was selected for the team to play
Argentina in our final warm-up game, and, unsurprisingly,
I had a nightmare. My World Cup hopes were hanging by
a thread.

I was later told by Gats that I had in fact been lucky
to make the party, and that I owed my place to the
unfortunate injury suffered by Morgan Stoddart. Stodds
had been looking phenomenal in training, but broke his
leg badly in our last warm-up match against England. He
never recovered from the injury, and it eventually forced
him to retire. It was such a shame for him. I'd first come
across him in my Llanelli days when he was playing for

Pontypridd. By now he'd developed into quite a player: I reckon he'd have gone on to win a hatful of Welsh caps and become a Lion, too.

As it was, in an eerie echo of the scene four years before, I was taken aside by Gats at our Vale HQ and told how the land lay. It was even in the same room where Nigel Davies had broken the news about my non-inclusion in the 2007 squad. This time, the news was better, if only owing to the ill fortune of my rival: 'Just to let you know, we weren't going to pick you for this World Cup. You knew that, didn't you?' asked Warren. 'Well, because of the injury to Stodds – you're going.' I couldn't say anything, really. Strictly on form, I was lucky to make the cut.

The good news was that the knee was finally settling down a bit, and I left for New Zealand determined to make up for lost ground. I didn't expect to be in the team for our opening game against South Africa in Wellington. The plan (as I understood it) was that I'd have another week of rehab before making my comeback against the Samoans. Hooky took the number 15 jersey for the Springbok game. He was unlucky the touch judges ruled that one of his kicks at goal had gone wide – it could have made a big difference to the outcome. Earlier, Toby (Taulupe) Faletau – a player I'd first noticed in Spala – scored a try. I remembered watching him out in Poland, gliding across the pitch like a gazelle, and thinking: 'This guy's immense, he's going to be world class.' He gave notice of his talent in that game, taking the fight to the South Africans with a barnstorming display. Even so, we came up short, beaten 17-16, and headed for Hamilton knowing we needed a result against a tough-looking Samoan side.

Looking back, perhaps I should have seen the writing on the wall. 'Well done, Halfers. Awesome kick, Halfers!' Howley would be shouting in training. The only time he'd speak to me would be to shout 'Byrney!' when he thought I'd done something wrong. Short of him telling me to fuck off home, he couldn't have made the pecking order much clearer. Still, my heart sank when Gats read out the team to face Samoa. It was the first time since becoming a Wales regular in 2008 that I'd been left out of a major game, for any reason other than injury.

We saw off the Samoans in a tight encounter. Leigh, in fairness, helped set up Shane's winning try. Victory meant the pressure was off for our next game – against Namibia in New Plymouth – a match we were expected to win easily. I was named in the starting side, and scored what turned out to be my last try in a Wales jersey, as we rattled up 80 points. But even that moment was marred by a run-in with the management. I'd passed the ball to Halfpenny in the build-up to the score, only for him to be tackled short of the line. He popped the ball up for me to cross instead. Afterwards, Jenks, a man with whom I'd always enjoyed a good rapport, joked: 'You knew what you were doing there, didn't you, Byrney, passing to Halfers early so he'd get tackled? You could have drawn the man and put him in.' I hoped he really was joking. After all the shit I'd had from Howley, I didn't want Jenks, a guy I'd always got on with, having a dig at me as well.

For the record, I didn't give the ball to Leigh early so he'd get tackled. I suppose I COULD have drawn the man, but we were 60 points up against Namibia. Unfortunately, Halfpenny was tackled and passed to me – end of story. But Jenks' comment – even if it was tongue in cheek – fed my growing feeling of paranoia.

Still, I kept my place in the team for the next match, back in Hamilton against Fiji. By this point we were playing really well, and put the Fijians to the sword, avenging our defeat of four years earlier. Considering the state of my knee (still swelling up like a balloon after every training session) I played well and did some good things. I thought 'I'm back into it, now.' Then, on 69 minutes, a message came down from the coaching box: 'Byrne onto the wing, Halfpenny to full back' 'That's strange,' I thought to myself. Halfpenny, after all, normally played on the wing when I was on the field. With hindsight, of course, the move was a dress rehearsal for what would happen the following week, when Leigh was handed the number 15 shirt for the quarter-final against Ireland. And, though I certainly didn't suspect this at the time, it also signalled my last moments in a Wales shirt.

Now don't get me wrong, here: I have no personal problem with Leigh Halfpenny. He's a lovely, lovely guy. Not the type of guy I'd go out for a post-match pint with, admittedly (he'd probably prefer a chocolate bar – each to his own) but I don't dislike him. I've never considered him to be a better full back than me, however. A good winger, certainly, but not in the Blanco or even, dare I say it, the Byrne mould as an attacking 15. For a season or so after he was first picked there for Wales, he could do no wrong in the eyes of the media: if he made a tackle, it was brilliant. Same if he took a high ball. But all full backs do those things. Aside from one effort against Australia for the Lions, I don't recall him making any breaks. Granted, given his size, he's brave in the tackle and good in the air. But, in my opinion, the only area where he truly trumped me was goal kicking. And that, I believe, is why I was ousted from the side.

Missing out on a World Cup quarter-final (again, I didn't make the bench) was devastating, naturally. My response was to go 'off tour' – that is, on the piss. Why not? It wasn't a case of sulking. I'm just of the mind that there's no point twiddling my thumbs in the hotel when there's no game to prepare for. I might as well go out and do something. Fortunately, there were others of a similar outlook: Aled Brew and Powelly, to name but two. We, together with the other reserves, were by now training in a separate group from the others. I'd roomed with Aled for much of the trip and we got on well, and Powelly, as I may have mentioned, is not a man who needs much convincing of the merits of a night out.

Wellington – match week – and we were on the piss the whole time. It was the same story the week after in Auckland. The fringe players from the France squad (our opponents for the semi-final) were in the same boat, and on the night before the big game, I was drinking with Fabrice Estebenez, one of those who were surplus to requirements. I suppose it wasn't the most responsible thing I've ever done – one injury and I may have been drafted into the match-day squad – but at the time I thought 'fuck it'. I sat down to watch the semi-final at Eden Park with a hangover.

Looking back, perhaps I was experiencing a sense of release after all the stuff that had been going on – the stress with my knee, the hassle from Howley. He was barely speaking to me by this point, by the way, although we did have a passing encounter in semi-final week. It was the Wednesday before the match. Thursday was to be a day off, so Brewey and I went on a bender in Auckland. The next morning, the hotel room was a scene of carnage: takeaway boxes, empty bottles, room-service trays littered the floor. Having got in at around 4 a.m., we were yet to surface when there came a knock at the door. 'Laundry Service. Would you like new towels?' asked a female voice. 'No, thank you,' I groaned from under the duvet. Ten minutes later there was another knock: 'New towels, sir?' 'No thanks,' I replied. Another ten minutes passed and a there was a third knock. I threw off the sheets and screamed: 'I told you: I don't want any FUCKING TOWELS!' This time it was a man's voice at the door, sounding none too impressed: 'Byrney! Open this door. It's ROB HOWLEY!'

Bollock naked, I waded through the debris of the previous night and opened the door. Rob was brandishing

a Wales shirt and marker pen: 'Sign this. You two are
the only ones I haven't got.' He was collecting signatures
for a signed jersey to give to a friend back in Bridgend.
I scribbled my name, and shuffled back into the room to
give it to Brewey, who was still in bed. Rob surveyed the
scene of debauchery. 'Good night last night, then, was
it?' he said, looking somewhat displeased. 'Nah... quiet
one, Rob,' I replied. Mentally, I added: 'That's my career
fucked.'

There was no point trying to mend fences now. We lost
– agonisingly – to France, and then it was time for the
'Fab Four' to embark on one final piss up, our last on a
rugby tour. It was an 'all dayer' to remember. We headed
to the Chapel Bar in the Auckland suburb of Ponsonby,
one of my favourite places. There, we sang 80s karaoke
songs and got stuck into the cocktail menu, before
playing 'credit card roulette' to decide who'd foot the bill.
Shane lost – twice – which cost him a fair bit of his tour
fee, but made it a cheap day for the rest of us!

I'm glad I went out in style. After all, for me
personally, the rugby had been a bit of a farce. It had
been my first, and last, World Cup, and, as it turned out,
my last hurrah as a Wales player. I never had the chance
to pull on that red jersey again. Or, at least, not until one
night in November 2013...

CHAPTER 10

La Chandelle

I'd always wanted to play for a foreign club. I was grateful to the Scarlets for giving me my chance as a professional, and I'd had some great times with the Ospreys, but the thought of getting out of Wales and experiencing the rugby and culture of another country had always appealed.

I'd first had the chance during the 2009 Lions tour, when South African franchise Western Stormers tried to sign me. Coach Rassie Erasmus had contacted my agent to say he'd been impressed with my performances; we met for coffee, and an offer was put on the table. I definitely would have gone. Playing in the Super 14, as it was then called, would have been great – not something many Welsh players have done. And, looking back, I'd already peaked in a Wales jersey by then, so I wouldn't have missed much in that respect. But the Ospreys wouldn't release me.

Then there was my brush with the NFL. OK, quite a brief brush, but a brush nonetheless. It was in 2010, not long after that famous Six Nations win over the Scots. My agent at the time, James Bulmer, got in touch to say NFL

Europe were scouting for talent, and did I fancy trying out as a punter? For those of you not acquainted with America's national winter sport, the punter is the guy who comes on when the team needs to kick the ball downfield and gain territory. He also takes kick-offs. It doesn't involve much contact, and you can carry on playing till you're 40. It sounded good to me, especially as word was that the Miami Dolphins were in the market for a punter.

So, off I went to Watford, where a guy from the NFL ran the rule over me, measuring my reaction times, the length and 'hang time' (height) of my kicks, and all the rest of it. I'd never kicked an American football before, and fluffed a few. But when I caught them right they were still going a fair distance. I didn't make the cut, though. When the NFL experts studied the footage, they reckoned my reaction times were a bit too slow: up against the speed merchants in the NFL, I'd have risked being charged down. Bye-bye, Miami.

France isn't quite Florida, weather-wise, but I'd always fancied playing there. As regards where, I had no particular preference... that is, till we visited one particular place with the Ospreys: ASM Clermont Auvergne. It was an eye-opening afternoon. Running out at Stade Marcel-Michelin, I had a feeling like I'd never experienced before outside international rugby. The atmosphere was spine tingling, the place packed to the rafters with partisan home support. Playing in front of 3–4,000 in Wales – no disrespect to the fans there – seemed a bit flat by comparison. I remember making a mental note:

'I wouldn't mind running out here as a home player.' It helped that I played well, putting Tommy Bowe in for a try, and winning the Man of the Match award, no easy feat on French soil. The powers that be must have taken note. Not long afterwards, Clermont made an offer. Unfortunately, my employers wanted more than they were prepared to pay, and I feared my chance was gone.

But with the Ospreys announcing cutbacks in 2011, I scented another opportunity. I had my agent contact Clermont and, to my delight, we were able to do a three-year deal, starting after the World Cup that year.

The city of Clermont-Ferrand sits surrounded by a ring of dormant volcanoes in the Massif Central region of France. Once a Roman settlement, now it's best known as the home of Michelin tyres. Because of its industrial heritage, the city has a strong working-class ethos, which was one of the reasons I liked it – it reminded me of my roots. Also, it's a bona fide rugby town. There is a soccer team – Clermont Foot 63 – but it's the oval ball that enjoys sporting supremacy.

Rugby is king in Clermont. There are over 10,000 season-ticket holders, and the remainder that go on sale are like gold dust. On match days, crowds will queue outside the ground from first light. The Clermontois constantly badger the players for tickets, and, as a foreigner, my allocation was usually going spare. One day, I popped into town to buy an iPhone, and gave the guy in the shop my pair. In return I got a free phone, and the bloke looked like he was about to shed tears of gratitude. He'd never been to a home match before, and this was his chance.

I arrived after the World Cup, and moved into a penthouse apartment. It was pretty swanky, with its own pool, but lonely too. I'd recently got engaged to Andrea, and it was tough leaving her behind in Wales. In my third season, she joined me in France, and we moved into a house near Volvic (where the mineral water comes from). But to begin with, there was little to do when I wasn't training or playing except to watch UK programmes on TV. Matters weren't helped by the inaccessibility of the place. To get there from Wales, you had to take two flights or three train journeys. However you tackled it, it was 12 hours each way: you can get to New York quicker.

Naturally, given the language barrier (made worse by my problems with dyslexia, which I'll return to later), I tended in general to be more comfortable socialising with the English-speaking players – like Kiwis Mike Delany, Benson Stanley and my old mate Regan King. Regan, in particular, was worth his weight in gold, translating all the calls for me on the training field. That said, I did strike up a great friendship with Frenchman Alexandre Lapandry. Andrea and I hung out with Alex and his girlfriend, spending evenings in his basement, where we'd drink wine and sample French delicacies like cheese and oysters. It was a far cry from the building-site days. I'd never had myself down as an espresso man, but after three years in France I couldn't get enough of the stuff.

We even went to Châteauneuf-du-Pape to see how they make the famous wine. So the secret's out: I became a bit of a culture vulture. Just don't tell them back on the Wildmill Estate.

Some of my South Walian dietary habits survived intact, however. One morning, at breakfast on one of our away trips, I went to put some tomato ketchup on my eggs. Being a council-estate boy, ketchup was a natural accompaniment to most meals – I'd have probably put it on my Sunday dinner! But the team doctor wasn't impressed, rushing over to lecture me on the ill effects on my body. All the Frenchmen dipping their bread in bowls of chocolate milk didn't seem to bother him.

Those away trips were hard work. Because of Clermont's remote location, they'd nearly all involve long coach journeys, some lasting up to seven hours. We'd set off the day before the game, stopping halfway to stretch our legs, before arriving at the hotel in the evening. The closest destination was Brive – a mere two-hour stretch – but an evening match at Biarritz was a serious slog, especially when you took the return journey into account. Let's say the game finished at 10 p.m., we'd be on the bus by 11, before driving through the night to get home.

It was far cry from the 'recovery protocols' I'd come to know in Wales. Back there, it was protein shakes all round, with an ice bath or maybe a spot of cryotherapy thrown in. In France, we'd tuck into four or five ham and cheese baguettes, then the doctor would come round doling out sleeping tablets, which we'd neck down with about a gallon of Heineken. We'd arrive back at Clermont at about 6 a.m., clear the coach of all the rubbish, and jump in our cars and head into town. There was a place called Café Del Sol that stayed open till 8 a.m. – if we were lucky, we'd make the last couple of hours. We were never short of options, anyway: two of the boys, Aurélien Rougerie and Thomas Domingo, owned bars.

Like I said before, the locals treated us like gods. This attitude even extended to those responsible for law and order, which helped get us out of a scrape one night. There was this club we used to go to, out on an industrial estate on the outskirts of the town. Being a bit out of the way, it was tempting to take the car and drive home afterwards. I'm not advocating drink driving. I certainly wouldn't do it at home, and I shouldn't have done it in France, either. But sure enough, I emerged from the club one night with South African Gerhard Vosloo – both of us well over the limit – and jumped in the car. We'd driven about 100 yards down the road when we were flagged down by a policeman. Noticing it was a club car, the officer bade us get out. 'Monsieur Byrne, Monsieur Vosloo!' he cried, relieving me of my keys and passing them to his sergeant. With that, he ushered Gerhard and me into his own vehicle and drove us back to my place. On arrival, he produced a bottle of whiskey and some cigars. Some hours and quite a few drinks later, he left to finish his shift.

*****

I didn't have to endure too many of the away trips, fortunately. In France, the priority – certainly as far as the league is concerned – is to win your home games. If you can nick two away results a season, and pick up a few losing bonus points here and there, you're more or less guaranteed a place in the top six and therefore the play-offs. That's why you'll see French players celebrating a narrow defeat like they've won the World Cup. It also meant most sides would field their fringe players for away fixtures; I reckon I only played about half of them per season. It was different with the Heineken Cup: by the time I got to Clermont, the club was taking that competition much more seriously. But, as most of those games were outside France, we'd charter a plane and avoid the dreaded coach journeys.

Playing at home was a different matter altogether. We were more or less unbeatable there. I only remember losing one home game in three years, and that was the last one I ever played: against Castres in the play-offs. Before that, the nearest we came to defeat was against Toulon one time. Jonny Wilkinson had dropped a goal with seconds remaining; but, from the restart, Matt Giteau gave away a penalty for deliberately knocking the ball into touch, and Brock James stepped up to slot the points. I guess a lot of our success was down to the passionate home support I've mentioned. The people in Clermont didn't have much money to spend, but what they had, they spent on rugby. Each week we'd hold an open training session in front of about 3,000 people, and afterwards we'd go round signing autographs and posing for pictures. It was a great idea, I thought – one we should adopt in Wales.

That family ethos extended to the club itself. Back in Wales you'd turn up on a Monday morning, say 'alright' to your mates, then sit in the corner and keep your head down. Here, you were expected to shake hands with everyone – not just fellow players and coaching staff, but the cleaners and receptionist, too. One day I forgot to shake someone's hand – they then asked me that evening: 'Lee – ça va? Why did you not shake my hand?' Thanks to Michelin's sponsorship, Clermont is a wealthy club, but it hasn't lost touch with its values.

That said, some of the players were mad, the forwards in particular. They needed to be, given the murderous approach of some of our opponents. One afternoon, I found myself at the bottom of a ruck at Stade Montois, a place far from civilisation and video refs. Suddenly, I felt this guy's fingers hooking onto the sides of my mouth and violently pulling sideways. I tried to bite down, but couldn't because of my gum shield. I could barely breathe, and was left with some nasty cuts. I thought it was poetic justice when the bloke who did it was given a good hiding by Andy Hazell, the Gloucester back row, the following season. On another occasion I was left needing 26 stitches after Florian Fritz used his forearm to remove my head from a ruck. In any other country it would have been a citing, no question.

Hanging round your own teammates wasn't much safer, mind. Hooker Benjamin Kayser once headbutted me in the dressnig room before a game. Others would slap you in the face. It was mental – but you couldn't say anything: it was just their unique way of getting everyone 'up' for the action.

Given such pre-match antics, it's probably unsurprising that the violence occasionally extended to the game itself. One mass brawl at Perpignan sticks in my mind. I kept a safe distance as the combatants spilled over into the advertising hoardings, the referee blowing his whistle frantically as he tried to regain control of proceedings. Suddenly, I heard an aggressive-sounding voice behind me: 'Come on then, butt!' It was Hooky, who'd recently signed for Perpignan. We fell about laughing, while the chaos continued to unfold nearby.

I wasn't amused by our pre-match warm-up routine, however. Franck Azéma (now the head coach at Clermont, but in those days in charge of the forwards) had us doing full-contact sessions on the pitch BEFORE the game. You could quite easily find yourself heading into the changing room with a dead leg, before you'd even started. Franck had apparently been a hard nut back in his own playing days, and evidently wanted some of that to rub off on us. His heart may have been in the right place, but personally, I thought he was a lunatic! In the end, I negotiated a gentleman's agreement with some of the others: we'd lay off the physical stuff... until the whistle went, at least.

*****

You could forgive me for being a bit paranoid about my fitness after all the trouble with my knee. Thankfully, the injury didn't flare up at Clermont, thanks largely to a new treatment I was having, known – to give it its technical name – as viscosupplementation. Every couple of months, I'd have an injection of chicken protein taken from the rooster's comb (that is, the bit on top of the bird's head) into the joint. This was expensive, about £500 a time, and there's no firm scientific evidence that it works – that said, it did seem to reduce the inflammation, and allowed me to play pain-free. I was never quite the same player I had been: my running gait had changed, and my pace was reduced – I'd say I was playing at about 80% of my 2008 peak. But, placebo effect or not, I'd say the chicken protein added three years to my career.

It also helped that I got on with the coach, Vern Cotter. Contrary to his dour demeanour in front of camera, Cotter was a really good guy: as hard as fuck, but prepared to give the boys some leeway. On Mondays, I'd usually turn up showing signs of the weekend's partying. As we shook hands, Vern would flare his nostrils and say: 'Byrney, were you on the piss on the weekend? You're stinking of vodka!' But he'd be laughing as he said it, and he'd still pick me. Touchingly, he also said he couldn't understand why I was being overlooked for national duty. 'Have you been shagging someone's wife over there? Do you want me to put in a good word in with Gatty?' I told him not to bother: I was enjoying my rugby where I was.

Like Gats, Vern – also a New Zealander – put a big emphasis on professionalism and fitness, something that didn't always come naturally to the French players. I used my contacts back home to help the club negotiate a deal with PAS, a supplier of dietary supplements. Suddenly, you'd see these big hairy French props gulping down protein shakes and looking none too impressed by the flavour. Not all of them were too keen on the gym, either.

For me, as a graduate of the Gatland school of hard work, all this training was par for the course. It came as a bit of a culture shock to the French boys, though. The gym hadn't really been their thing before – they'd preferred instead to rely on natural talent. To be fair, of that there was no shortage. Flanker Julien Bonnaire was an absolute machine on the field, and the likes of Parra and Fofana as talented as you'd wish to find. With their tails up, they were unstoppable. At the same time, I felt there was some truth in the old cliché about the French and their mental frailty. If we were 15 nil down in a game, even early on, I'd sense heads going down around me. It wasn't weakness, exactly. Clermont's exemplary record in Europe gives the lie to the old myth about the French being poor travellers: you don't beat the likes of Leinster or Exeter away by being flaky. But perhaps, in the very biggest games, the top three inches let us down.

I was convinced it was largely down to the club's

woeful record in big finals. They'd lost umpteen domestic ones (although I'm delighted to say they won the 2017 title), and it was the same in Europe, where, so far, the ledger reads: three final appearances, three defeats. The club insists there's no mental baggage, but all those losses must have had an effect. I think Benjamin Kayser has been on the losing side in at least four Heineken Cup Finals for various teams.

We certainly didn't lack for firepower out wide. On one wing we had the giant Fijian Napolioni Nalaga, and on the other, another guy of Fijian extraction – Sitiveni Sivivatu. Sivivatu was a dazzling talent: the sort who could beat a man for fun and make rugby look easy. Along with Shane, I'd say he's the best winger I've played with. He also had very exacting standards. Not long after we started playing together, he took me into the video room and gave me a lecture about my positioning. 'This is what you should be doing,' he said, pointing out my errors. Bear in mind that by this point I'd won 46 caps and been on a Lions tour – I admit I was somewhat taken aback. But, after reflecting on what he'd said, I realised it made sense. I thanked him later, and the pep talk certainly did the trick. Not long afterwards, against the Scarlets in a European game, I scored a great try on the loop around off him.

Sivi may have been a model pro, but he also knew how to relax. In common with the other Fijian boys at Clermont, he had a very particular way of doing it, in fact. It was called Kava, a favourite beverage in the South Seas – definitely not to be confused with the Cava that you

get in Tesco's. This particular drink is a sedative, so has
the opposite effect to that generally wrought by alcohol
on rugby players. The more you drink, the mellower you
become. A Kava session with the Fijians would generally
end with everyone sitting around, saying nothing.
Definitely different to a night out with the Bridgend boys
back home.

This wasn't the only substance I experimented with
in France. Don't worry, I'm not about to lift the lid
on some dalliance with illicit substances. I'm talking
about Zopiclone, a sleeping medication. You remember
I mentioned the doctor coming round on the bus with
sleeping tablets? Well, that's what they were. To start
with, I'd sought the medication out for entirely legitimate
reasons. I was in a new country, missing Andrea, and
living on my own, with little to do apart from train and
play. The medication would at least help me get a decent
night's sleep. But, over time, I – and others – discovered
that the tablets had a potent effect when combined with
booze. You'd neck a few with the beer, and soon enough
the world would go all fluffy and fuzzy... just like your
recollections the following day. At Clermont, we worked
out where the doctor kept his stash. He soon realised
we were pilfering his pills and moved them, only for the
cycle to repeat itself.

Using sleeping pills for recreational purposes is,
of course, not what they're designed for, and I'm not
condoning it. But we certainly weren't the first rugby
players to seek a high in this way. It's apparently quite

a big thing in the Southern Hemisphere. All Black pair
Cory Jane and Israel Dagg admitted publicly to taking
them before going drinking in 2011, and there's also
been a problem with them in Australian rugby league. It's
not sensible, of course. People die after mixing sleeping
pills and alcohol, even before you consider the risk of
becoming addicted to them. I should know: it wouldn't be
long before I found myself using Zopiclone again – this
time after a nasty shoulder injury at the Dragons.

*****

There was nothing sleepy about our performances on
the field. With the likes of Sivivatu, Fofana, Bonnaire and
Parra, that Clermont team was probably the best I've
played in, talent-wise. Which made our failure to actually
win anything while I was there all the more disappointing.

We came desperately close, of course, particularly in
the Heineken Cup. In my first season, we were narrowly
beaten in the semi-finals by Leinster, the eventual
champions. Fofana could have won it for us at the death,
but lost the ball on the line – he was in tears afterwards.
But he was on fire the following season, helping us reach
the final in Dublin. Standing between us and glory were
our arch-rivals Toulon.

It had felt like our year: we'd stormed through the
competition, playing the best rugby, and led for most
of the final as well. But Delon Armitage's late score

(the Clermont fans never forgave him for his gloating celebration) snatched the dream away. It was the most disappointing defeat of my career. Afterwards, I sat on the pitch in stunned disbelief, watching our opponents celebrate. Up in the stand – where my family and friends were among the travelling fans – the tears flowed. Ask any sportsman and they'll tell you finishing second is no consolation – particularly when the margin of defeat is so narrow. Andrea had to retrieve my runners-up medal after I'd tossed it away.

I guess we just hadn't known how to close the game out. By contrast, Toulon – who hadn't played anywhere near as well as us that season – were staffed by gnarly old pros, the likes of Wilkinson (who kicked 11 points in the final), Giteau and Bakkies Botha... serial winners, who never knew when they were beaten.

I'm glad to say Clermont is finally shedding its reputation for choking on the big stage. In the summer of 2017, I sat down at a bar in New Zealand (where I was covering the Lions Tour for talkSPORT) and watched my old club clinch only their second ever Top 14 title, beating our old nemesis Toulon in the process. Finally, the monkey seems to be off our backs, and I couldn't be happier for the boys. Let's hope a European title is next.

2014 was the closest I came to getting my hands on some silverware in France, and to joining the select band of Welshmen to win the Heineken Cup (I still think of it as the Heineken Cup, by the way: 'Champions' Cup just doesn't quite cut it, somehow). The next year we reached the last four again, but got thumped 46-6 by Saracens. It felt like the end of an era – and for me, it was. Not long afterwards, my time as a Clermont player came to an end. I'd loved it. Yes, I'd had my problems with the language, and I regretted not being able to have a laugh with the French boys in their mother tongue. But, as a cultural and rugby experience, it was the highlight of my career. I was playing with great players in front of great fans, and relished being out of the infamous Welsh 'goldfish bowl'. The social life was amazing, and we returned home with two additions to the family: a pair of schnauzer puppies called Hank and Marcy.

And, by the way, just in case you were wondering about the chapter title: 'La Chandelle' is a French term for 'up-and-under', and the nickname the Clermont supporters gave me. Literally, it means 'candle'. My teammates would shout it when I raised a glass with them after the game.

When it comes to Clermont, for me the flame will always burn brightly.

CHAPTER 11

Dyslexia and Me

Promising sporting careers have been cut short my many things: an inopportune injury, an over-fondness for partying, selectorial whim. But I've never heard of anyone who nearly failed to make the grade because he couldn't understand his own team's play-sheets.

Fundamentally, rugby is a simple game, whatever level you play at. But the better the standard, the more ways there are to complicate it. When I was playing for Bridgend Athletic in Division 5, we generally had one backs move: a 'miss two' straight to me. When I moved to Tondu, things got a bit more complicated, and when I turned pro with the Scarlets, trickier still. By the time I was playing international rugby, remembering all the different plays became the rough equivalent of rocket science – well, for me, anyway.

You hear people talk about big match nerves, the pressure of performing on the big stage. For me, by far the most nerve-racking, stomach-churning aspect of life as a rugby player was learning the calls. This was where my dyslexia, usually well disguised around my fellow professionals, came back to haunt me. I never feared an opponent, but I was petrified of forgetting a call. It was the worst thing about training and playing. I would dread the bus journey to the ground before big games. All that would be going through my head was the calls. The irony was we'd only ever use one or two, but we'd have to have about 20 'in the locker' – just in case. I've already mentioned how Shaun Edwards spotted my pre-match nervousness and gave me books to read. I remember one particularly well: it was called *Hurricane*, and was all about the American boxer Rubin Carter. The trouble was I never reached the end – Tom Shanklin jokes that I was reading the same book for five years!

I had a few tricks up my sleeve to help me mask the problem. During Wales training, there'd always be two full backs. When we'd first run a move, I'd pretend to be stretching or doing up my laces so I could watch the reserve do it; then I'd know where to run when it was my turn. I'd also print out the play sheets and pin them up at home. There'd be about 15 of them stuck up around the house; above the toilet, on the fridge, above the bathroom mirror. The place must have resembled the den of some mad scientist. But, even after all that, I'd still panic during the game. I'd be on the pitch at the Millennium Stadium, shouting to Shanklin or Mark Jones to tell me where I should be standing. They must have wondered what the hell was going on.

Doing concussion tests was also embarrassing. Following a head knock, one of the exercises the doctors made you do was to recite the alphabet backwards off a chart. I had problems reading it forwards, let alone in reverse! In the end, I'd cheat by writing the letters down on the back of my hand.

The whole issue escalated when I moved to France. After I joined Clermont, the club paid for weekly French lessons for me and the other overseas players. These I soon came to dread. As I've described above, being a rugby player didn't entirely protect me from dyslexia, but at least I was in an environment where I felt comfortable. The French lessons transported me back to my schooldays and the miseries of the classroom. I could barely get to grips with grammar in English, never mind French, and I quickly fell behind. I was forced discreetly to tell our teacher what the problem was: after that, he started giving me private tuition. The upshot was I never learned to speak the language. I could understand what was being said to me, but found replying impossible. The situation improved when Andrea arrived for my last season. By that stage I could understand everything and – with her being able to speak decent French – between us we got by.

This was not only embarrassing, but could cause problems with some of my French teammates. I'm sure they thought I just couldn't be bothered. 'Parlez français,' they'd say, reminding me I was in their country now. They could get a bit nasty about it. But I was too embarrassed to admit the truth, to them or the coaches. In the alpha-male rugby environment, I presumed dyslexia would not be considered a valid excuse for my failings with the language. Luckily, Regan King was on hand to help me learn the calls on the training field. But away from rugby, I fear they viewed me as a typical foreign mercenary – there purely to take the money, while refusing to engage with the culture around me.

*****

At its worst, I actually thought dyslexia was going to stop me from playing professional rugby altogether. But, looking back on my career, my condition has been a double-edged sword. For all the difficulties I had in processing and remembering information, I came to realise that my visual-spatial awareness was much better than average. In layman's terms, I was able to think in pictures. I've since been told this is a common phenomenon among dyslexics. A dyslexic plumber, for instance, might be able to recall the layout of your water pipes despite not having visited your house for years – all thanks to an excellent visual memory. It was a similar thing for me on the field. I felt I had an almost uncanny eye for gaps, an ability to see what was happening before it actually happened. The try I scored against Australia in 2008 was a classic example.

School learning is traditionally done by rote, in a linear way – exactly what dyslexics struggle with. Looking back, my school career followed the classic path of someone with the condition. I couldn't understand what I was being taught so I became frustrated and disruptive, and was then perceived as stupid or lazy. The truth is, my brain's just wired differently. Some people's brains are predominantly left-sided, meaning they're more logical, while others, including dyslexics, are biased to the right side, which means they're more creative and visual in their thinking. Famous sufferers include Albert Einstein and Bill Gates. I'm not saying I'm about to become an astrophysicist or the next Silicon Valley billionaire. But learning about the leading lights who have shared my condition has certainly helped me to view it more positively.

Fortunately, it seems that education has moved on since my schooldays, and dyslexia is now better understood. That's partly thanks to the work of certain charities, one of which I'm privileged to be involved with. Tomorrow's Generation is the brainchild of Anders Hedlund, a Swedish businessman based in Cardiff. Anders is a millionaire who employs more than 3,000 people worldwide in his gift-wrap and greetings-cards business. He's also dyslexic. After watching his son, who also has the condition, struggle in class (though with specialist tuition, he later got top A Levels), Anders decided to start a school for sufferers. With the help of rugby charity Wooden Spoon Wales, the Tomorrow's Generation learning centre was born.

I got in touch with the charity via social media, and they invited me to visit the centre in Cardiff. I'm now a trustee, and I can't speak highly enough of the work they do there. Currently, they offer support days to help dyslexic kids with literacy and numeracy, plus one-to-one tuition and holiday schools. The ultimate aim is for it to become a full-time centre, and for other units to open around the country. It's great to see what's going on there. I hope the kids look at me – and the thousands of other dyslexics who've done well in their fields – and see that you can succeed after all.

For me, coming to terms with my condition has been an important part of a wider transition: from rugby player to ex-rugby player. When I retired, Julie Paterson at the WRU got in touch to ask me if I'd be interested in sitting some tests designed to help former players adjust to life after rugby. One of them was the Myers-Briggs Type Indicator, a personality test designed to show how an individual thinks and what their strengths and weaknesses are. Not surprisingly, owing to the dyslexia I scored very low in some categories. But the test also helped me to understand the areas where I could do well – for instance the media and coaching.

Not for the first time, I have to thank my wife for helping me with all of this. Had it been left to me, I would no doubt have continued as I had previously in my career, muddling along and sweeping my dyslexia under the carpet. But after seeing how I'd struggled out in France, she encouraged me to seek help. That's how I came to meet Anne Rees, the specialist in Cardiff who diagnosed me. Slowly, with Andrea's support, I came to realise my condition was nothing to be ashamed of.

She even persuaded me to make a programme for ITV Wales about the condition, entitled *Dyslexia and Me*. During filming, I returned to see Anne, and we talked on camera about my experiences. I was starting to understand that while the learning difficulty had caused problems, in other ways it had been a big positive.

And that's how I view dyslexia now: something that's helped me get where I am today. Recently, Tomorrow's Generation sent me a drawing done by one of the kids. It was of me, in rugby kit, and underneath it said: 'My inspiration'. If being open about dyslexia inspires one child to have a happier life, I'd say it's been well worth the effort.

CHAPTER 12

Desperate Dragons

I was peering out through the window of the gym in Ystrad Mynach. Outside, it was pissing down with rain. Lyn was taking backs training, and balls were going down left, right and centre as I watched. I was six months into rehabilitation after shoulder surgery, but still several more away from returning to action. A year earlier I'd been basking in the French springtime, getting ready for the Heineken Cup Final; now I was in South Wales in the rain, at a club going nowhere fast. I was starting to think I'd made a mistake.

Joining the Dragons had seemed like a good idea at the time. I'd had three great seasons at Clermont, and there was talk of me being offered another. Bordeaux were also interested. But it was time to come home. I had an amazing wife who'd put her broadcasting career on hold to spend a year with me in France: it was time to put her first. And, as much as I'd enjoyed my French adventure, I missed my family and friends in Wales.

The Dragons – despite being seen as fourth in the pecking order of the Welsh regions – seemed like a good fit. My old Ospreys boss Lyn Jones had taken over the coaching reins, and the deal on offer was attractive: alongside Taulupe Faletau, I was set to be the highest earner at the club. As an added sweetener, they even offered me the captain's armband. I'd never skippered a side before, not even as a kid. But after 46 caps and my experiences on the big stage in France, I had no hesitation. I felt I had plenty of leadership qualities to offer a young Dragons squad.

In many ways, my first impressions of the place were positive. These were the days before Newport County started playing at Rodney Parade, and the much-maligned playing surface was in good condition. The new gym and pitches at Ystrad Mynach were impressive, although training on the artificial surface was torture for my knee. Fitness guys Ryan Harris and Simon Church were excellent, as were the physios and most of the staff. But it soon became clear that there were some major flaws in the Dragons' operation.

Resources were much scarcer than they had been at Clermont. To a point, I'd expected this. But it was still a surprise to find that there was even a cap on how much tape we could use to strap up our knees. In France, there'd been an entire team of physios and doctors allocated to working with the first-team squad, but here, I soon got impression that the expertise we had was being spread too thinly. It was a situation that was to have major consequences for me later.

The coaching set-up also left a lot to be desired. Lyn

was an excellent forwards coach and, as I've previously described, a great innovator, but he was no backs guru. And yet, at the Dragons, he took responsibility for our attacking play. I felt for our young players. We had some promising talent in the back line – the likes of Tyler Morgan, Jack Dixon, Tom Prydie and Angus O'Brien – but, with respect, Lyn was not the right person to take charge of their development.

Although these issues concerned me, I put them to the back of my mind as we prepared for the season. Physically, I was OK – or at least as good as I was going to be, given my battered body. Thanks to the chicken protein injections, there were no new problems with my knee. I was also enjoying the captaincy side of things, and I think the youngsters were surprised by how approachable I was. Maybe, because I'd achieved a bit in the game, they expected some kind of big-time attitude. That was never going to happen. Whether playing for Bridgend Athletic or the British and Irish Lions, I like to think I've always stayed the same: a down-to-earth guy.

I enjoyed my first outing as skipper, even though we suffered a narrow defeat at Connacht. Then came our first home match in the Pro12: a Welsh derby against the Ospreys, my old team. Not long in, their winger Eli Walker went through, with just me to beat. I put an arm out to tackle him... and felt something pop. It was a disappointing end to my home debut. I was assessed at St Joseph's Hospital in Newport, where they told me I'd suffered a labrum tear in my left shoulder. The medics advised a week's rest, after which I'd be OK to resume playing. Being captain – and given our dicey start – Lyn was understandably keen to get me back on the field.

I missed our loss to Glasgow and returned to training the following week. But the pain wasn't getting easier. I couldn't lift weights, and it hurt every time I made a tackle. I had to visit the hospital for a cortisone injection before my comeback game, a routine repeated before the next three matches. Things weren't much better away from the field. At night, the burning pain in my shoulder left me struggling to sleep without the aid of medication.

In spite of everything, I put in a good performance to help us beat Stade Français in the European Challenge Cup – a fantastic result away from home, and the first time I felt I'd given the fans a glimpse of my capabilities – even though I was operating at only about 40% of my best. But, after the next game against Newcastle, still with no sign of improvement in my shoulder, Andrea persuaded me to seek a second opinion. This time, the doctors diagnosed a 10 cm tear in the rotator cuff. It appeared that playing on had exacerbated the original injury: instead of eight weeks out, I was now looking at eight months.

I'd say playing those extra games shortened my career by up to two years. I'm sure that at any other club, I'd have been taken out of the fray, operated on, and been back within a matter of months. I can only assume it was all to do with money: I was the second-highest earner at the club, and the top brass obviously wanted to see me on the field, not the treatment table.

Ro Kulkarni, the Dragons team doctor – also a board member at the region, and a big mate of Lyn's – oversaw my weekly painkilling injections at St Joseph's Hospital. One week, during my procedure, Ro popped to the toilet, leaving me to chat with the guy doing the injection. 'How's it looking?' I asked. 'How's it looking?' he replied. 'It's looking like you've got a massive tear in there.'

I have no proof that the senior people at the region knew the extent of my injury, but surely the fact I was having painkilling injections each week must have suggested all was not well. Not once was I shown a scan result by the medical team. Sadly, I'm not the only player to have ended his days at Rodney Parade in controversial circumstances. Andrew Coombs, another whose career was cut short by injury, was left with thousands of pounds' worth of medical bills after the region cancelled his insurance. The Dragons insisted they'd done nothing wrong in his case. For me, though, my treatment summed up the standards at Newport at the time. On a scale of 1– 10 for how I was treated, I'd say Clermont scored 10, the Dragons 1. Recently, I read some comments attributed to Lyn in the press, where he said players in France were treated 'like pieces of meat'. I found that ironic, given how I'd been managed at Rodney Parade.

I now found myself in a sticky situation – only two months into a two-year contact, and facing the prospect

of missing the rest of the season. By the time I was
due to be back on the field, I'd be 35. No one was
more frustrated than me – especially after I'd been
made captain – but there was little to do except have
the operation and get on with my rehab. At home,
things were strained. I had to sleep in a single bed for
six months, and was dosed up on anti-inflammatories
and painkillers. But it quickly became clear that my
unavailability was not sitting well with Lyn. Despite that
excellent European win in France, we'd lost six of our
eight games, and he was feeling the pressure.

I started to notice he was ignoring me around the club.
For the next four or five months he didn't say a word to
me. I could understand Lyn's frustration, but it was hardly
my fault – in fact, you could argue he'd made matters
worse by putting pressure on me to play when I was
obviously not right. Yet here he was, blanking me in the
corridors. One time I was in the gym, working my arse off
on the bike next to Jack Dixon, another injured player. By
now, it had been several months since Lyn had spoken to
me. Suddenly he walked in. Surely, I thought, he'll break
the silence this time. Instead, he went: 'Alright Jack,
how's it going? How long have you got left?' They chatted
for a moment before Lyn walked out, ignoring me.

Not long after this, I had my moment of clarity. To be
fair, there were some talented players at the Dragons
(that season we made the semi-finals of the European
Challenge Cup), but in the league we were mired in
mid-table mediocrity, and, as I said before, the overall

standards of professionalism were not exactly what I'd become used to. To make matters worse, I was nearing six months on the sidelines, after which it was written into my contract that the club wouldn't have to pay me any more. I still didn't have full flexibility in my shoulder (to this day I can't raise it beyond the horizontal) and there was no guarantee when I'd be coming back, if at all.

It was time to make a decision.

The next week, I invited Lyn to my house in Bridgend. I informed him that I wanted to quit, and proposed a deal which would see them buy me out of my second year. I'd written down what I considered to be a fair figure, one that would compensate me for loss of earnings while saving the club a few quid too. But when I handed it to Lyn, he gave it only a cursory look before commenting on how nice my coffee was. I asked him what he thought of my offer. He laughed, told me to come back to him when I'd come up with something more sensible, and left.

At least, I thought, I'll have my insurance money to fall back on. This was the tax-free sum that I was due to receive for a career-ending injury. I'd been sold the policy by a guy called Paul Morgan – an ex-Wales rugby league international and a bit of a wheeler-dealer – but an alright bloke. Being in my thirties, my premium had been expensive but I'd gone ahead and put it on the credit card. I'd also had to fill out an injury declaration form, detailing all the problems I'd had in my career thus far. I'd left nothing out: nine knee operations, the foot injury in 2009, up to and including a shoulder dislocation I'd suffered in France the previous season. Everything was faithfully reported.

A few months after my injury, I rang Paul and asked him to send me over a copy of my insurance certificate. We arranged to meet in Bridgend, and I brought my solicitor friend Dan Williams along to advise. But when Paul arrived, he was empty-handed. I asked him where the certificate was – he just muttered something about being unable to access it on his phone because there was no wi-fi. Later, it became clear he'd only taken out the policy after I'd told him about my injury, backdating the certificate accordingly.

With the Dragons refusing to pay me off, I was now facing the prospect of ending up seriously out of pocket. Paul tragically died of a brain haemorrhage shortly after our meeting, but fortunately for me, we unearthed an e-mail trail proving that I had indeed paid for my insurance policy before the season started. Despite this, actually getting the money proved a nightmare. For the best part of a year and a half, I was going back and forth between solicitors, spending plenty on legal advice for little return. Eventually, Andrea suggested we contact the Financial Ombudsman. He wrote back to say that he'd looked at my case and thought I'd been treated disgracefully, adding that he'd be contacting the policy underwriters on my behalf. Within two weeks they'd settled in full: I finally received the pay-out earlier this year, 18 months after I should have had it.

It was just another hassle in what proved a very stressful period. I wasn't the first and won't be the last to find retiring from rugby difficult. On top of that, there'd been the stress of chasing my insurance money and the negotiations with the Dragons, added to which I'd been hit with a huge tax bill from France. I'd also lost Jerry Collins – one of my best mates – in a car crash, and my sister was fighting cancer. That September, the eyes of the rugby world were on the World Cup. I was a recently-retired player with an uncertain future, and I was struggling to cope.

The extent to which I'd been affected by all the problems soon revealed itself. I was watching Andrea host an awards ceremony in Cardiff, sitting in the front row not far away from members of the Cardiff Blues team, when I suddenly felt very strange indeed. I started seeing flashing lights, and everything around me went purple. I dashed out of the room and ran outside, where I was sick. I couldn't face going back in and drove home to Bridgend, texting Andrea to let her know what had happened. I had no idea what was going on – frankly, I thought I might be dying.

The next day, I went to my GP and explained what had happened. Physically, I was fine: they told me I'd had a panic attack brought on by stress. It wasn't the first time I'd experienced such an episode. Following the Lions tour, I'd gone off to Las Vegas on holiday with a group of players including Mike Phillips, Gordon D'Arcy and Tommy Bowe. After several days of heavy drinking, one morning

I suddenly felt gripped by a terrible feeling of anxiety. Without saying anything to the others, I took myself off to the airport and bought a ticket to LA, where my girlfriend at the time was staying. On the plane, tossing and turning in my sleep, I knocked a cup of coffee over the businessman sitting next to me, staining his suit. When we landed, I bought him a new one at the airport. Looking back, the feelings which preceded that episode were very similar to those I was experiencing now: total panic and a feeling that I was going to die.

That time, the feelings had passed. On this occasion, I found myself sliding into a deep depression. I'd never been one to find getting out of bed difficult, but now I just couldn't see the point. I'd get up with Andrea, tell her I planned to do this or that, then go back to bed till 2 p.m. The gym in my garage, always a favourite refuge, went unused. I'd walk in, maybe sit on the bike for two minutes, and walk out again. There seemed nothing to stay in shape for. After I'd done the Myers-Briggs assessment, I'd been told of the importance of networking and making sure I was on people's radar. But I was afraid to go to events in case I had a panic attack. Naturally, the invitations started to dry up. This in turn fed my sense of despondency. But I just couldn't face the prospect of going to events and having to put on a brave face.

The booze didn't help. I'd always liked a pint, but without the structure I'd had in my playing days, the drink just made me feel worse. I started spending more time in London, on one occasion going to visit my old pal, Thom Evans. We spent all day on the piss, first at The Ship in Wandsworth, then at nightclub Boujis, the swanky spot once frequented by Princes William and Harry. The next morning, I had a job to do in a voice-over studio. It was before the World Cup, and I'd been asked to record a message to be played over the loudspeaker at Cardiff Central Train Station: something along the lines of welcoming people to Cardiff and asking them to make their way to the doors. The trouble was, owing to my dyslexia, I couldn't read the autocue. I had about ten goes at it, before the producer suggested we go upstairs to a quieter studio. I couldn't do it there either. In the end we had to give up, and I left with the message unrecorded.

The next day, I had a call from the guy at the agency that had offered me the work. He said that he'd heard I was reeking of drink when I turned up at the studio. I felt embarrassed and humiliated. I apologised, and told him about my dyslexia. It was particularly awkward since I'd already been paid. Kindly, they let me keep my fee (a grand for an hour's work), but I'd blown any hopes of working with them again.

You'd think I'd have been on safer ground when offered the chance to do some corporate hospitality Q and A sessions during the Rugby World Cup in 2015. But even then, my heart wasn't in it. I couldn't face watching the games and so would talk rubbish when questioned by the punters at half time. Because I knew my rugby, I think I pulled it off. But it said a lot about my state of mind.

At the time, I must have been a nightmare to be around at home. Once again, Andrea was my rock. She encouraged me to visit my GP, who prescribed me with Sertraline, an antidepressant. To begin with, I lied to her about taking the tablets. I'd always prided myself on being mentally tough, and I didn't like the idea of having to rely on medication. I thought I could pull through on my own – the truth was, I couldn't. I have to say the pills have helped: I'm still taking them now.

I really don't want to come across like I'm moaning here – another privileged sportsman/celebrity with a tale of woe. I'm very aware of how lucky I've been. And I wouldn't want you to think I'm laying claim to these problems as a sort of fashion accessory – something to make me appear more interesting, or to sell this book. I can only say that my depression and anxiety felt very real, and certainly affected my quality of life. Medication helped, as did seeing Lisa Harrison, a psychologist to whom I was referred by Anders at the dyslexia charity. She told me that depression was often sparked by stressful life events, like losing a job, the death of a loved one or a family illness. I'd experienced all of them in a six-month period – my body couldn't cope. A big part of the problem was, I suppose, finding a new direction in life now rugby had finished. For the last 12 years I'd lived the dream as a professional sportsman. Now here I was: 35, with no qualifications, having to start again from scratch.

I spent much of our first session in tears, but talking to Lisa definitely helped. So did getting involved with State of Mind, a charity that helps sports people with emotional problems. One of the trustees is Danny Sculthorpe, the ex-Rugby League player whose difficulties following retirement led him to contemplate suicide. Thankfully, I never reached that point, but it was comforting to read about his experiences and recovery. Duncan Bell, the ex-England prop, and one of the first to go public about depression, got in touch too. In the same way that dyslexia had been swept under the carpet in the macho world of rugby, so I suppose had mental health. Hopefully, thanks to the good work of State of Mind and other charities, that's now changing.

As I've already mentioned, the Myers-Briggs test had shown me the outlines of a path I might be able to follow. Now that my self-belief was starting to return, I was able to get out there and do something about it. For a long time, I'd lost confidence in what I'd achieved in my career. As I've said before, I was never an ultra-confident type at the best of times, and when I was struggling, my natural reticence ballooned into a full-blown inferiority complex. I couldn't see why anyone would care about what I'd done in my career. Now I'm myself again, I'm more likely to put things up on social media – tries I've scored, great wins I've been involved in, stuff like that. Why not? No one else will blow your trumpet for you, after all.

It had been a tough period, and obviously not the way I'd have wanted my playing career to end. The experience at the Dragons had been disappointing, and I didn't get a payoff from them at all, in the end. My injury and departure had also ruined my relationship with Lyn. Yes, he said some nice things about me when I retired, but I felt it was a bit late by then. When I'd really needed him, he wasn't there. If I saw him now, I'd walk on by.

That said, I got on fine with most of the staff and players at the Dragons. Occasionally, in my role as media pundit, I return to Rodney Parade to cover matches. In common with everyone else in Welsh rugby, I haven't enjoyed watching their struggles in recent seasons. Hopefully, they can turn a corner now the WRU have taken over the running of the region. Gwent has always been a great hotbed of the game in Wales, after all. We can't afford not to take advantage of the talent there.

CHAPTER 13

Train well, Play well

Early on a Sunday morning or on a day off, particularly towards the start of my career, you'd have been able to find me running up and down the sand dunes at Merthyr Mawr, near my home. The weather conditions didn't matter. In fact, when it was cold, dark and wet, I liked it even more. The important thing is that I was there, doing the extra yards – the hard graft which, I firmly believed, would give me the edge over my rivals. It would make me feel good, that thought: that while I was outside in the dark, lungs burning, they'd be lying in bed. I felt certain the hard work would pay off.

I'd always been interested in fitness. It started when I was a teenager: I would go to Bridgend Rec with my friends from the estate – the likes of 'Sticks' (Mark Florence) and Carl Tozer – to do weights. Pec deck, bicep curls, things like that. The whole aim at that point was to look good in a T-shirt. Then, after I met Brendan Roach, it became about more than just vanity. Fitness, for me, was a passion and a source of pride. I'd feel much more confident if I ran onto the field feeling like I'd had a good week of training behind me.

At every club I played for, I took a special interest in the physical work we did. I would question the fitness coaches – probably to the point of becoming a pain in the arse – asking them why we were doing such-and-such a routine, or had they considered trying this or that. I worked with some excellent ones: the likes of Mike McGurn at the Ospreys and his successor, Mark Bennett. Scott Crean at Clermont was also very good. For Wales, Canadian Dan Baugh was a real 'header' (nutter) – in a good way. Wayne Proctor of the Scarlets was probably the hardest of the lot: an absolute fucking animal. He'd hammer you for hour after hour. Looking back though – and this is no criticism of Procs – doing 3Ks and the like probably wasn't the most suitable thing for us. Since then, the science around rugby training has evolved massively.

Things really changed under Gats, I suppose. First, he brought in Craig White, a northerner with a background in rugby league. Craig got me in great shape for the Lions tour in 2009. I'd been off the field with my foot injury; but during the lay-off he helped to get me to another level, fitness-wise. By the time returned to the field in South Africa, I was flying.

Another Northerner, Paul Stridgeon – or 'Bobby', as he's known – was introduced to us on that Lions trip. Paul, previously with the England team and Toulon, has recently become national Consultant Head of Physical Performance for Wales. He certainly knows his stuff, and he also happens to be the most nuts bloke I've ever met.

One of his favourite party tricks is the 'human flag', a routine that involves grabbing onto a lamppost or similar object and hanging, body parallel to the ground, like a flag. It takes amazing strength (which, being a former freestyle wrestler, he had), and none of the players could do it.

Paul would do his flag trick wherever we went in South Africa, including on the street. Except one time it backfired. One day, we were relaxing in the hotel pool after training, and he spotted a lamp-post nearby. An ideal opportunity, thought Bobby, for the flag performance. 'Boys, boys – watch this,' he said. Except the post was plastic, not metal, and snapped under his weight. It was one of the funniest things I'd ever seen, particularly when he got up from the floor and walked off as if nothing had happened.

'Bobby' also – and there's no delicate way to put this – has a massive cock. I mention this because he had a tendency to unveil it at surprising moments. Like when we were doing weights in the gym. There I'd be, doing a bench press or a power clean or whatever – with a serious-faced Bobby watching on – only to look down and see his not-insignificant penis protruding from the leg of his shorts. Sometimes, while you were pumping iron, he'd slap you with it! This didn't do much for your concentration... but would provoke howls of mirth from any watching teammates.

None of which is to say he wasn't serious about his

work. His record shows he knew how to get results, but the humour and fun he brought to proceedings gave the boys a huge lift. Each week, he'd award the 'Bobby Cup' to the best-performing player. He'd also film funny home videos that would be shown at team meetings, one of which featured Paddy O'Reilly, or 'Rala', the Irish kit man. Bagmen being a notoriously lazy breed, the video featured Bobby walking into Rala's room to inquire after the whereabouts of the rugby balls. Inside, the camera revealed 'yer man' lying on the bed, wearing sunglasses, pretending to smoke what appeared to be a massive reefer (actually a rolled up newspaper). The video brought the house down. Amid the intensity of a Lions tour, lighter moments are so important. And that's where Bobby came into his own: he was always on a high.

After Craig White left the Wales set-up in 2010, we worked with an Australian guy called Adam Beard. Adam was a more serious character, but equally effective. In 2011, he oversaw our infamous World Cup preparations, including the trip to Spala and its notorious cryotherapy chambers. He also came up with this routine called the Watt Test (not to be confused with the test of the same name done by cyclists), one of the most painful things I've ever done, and dreaded by all the boys. It comprised eight sprints, with 15 seconds of recovery between each. From a lying position, you'd have to sprint 5 m out to a cone and back, before doing the same with one 30 m out. The whole thing only lasted four minutes or so, but it was four minutes of pure hell. By about the third set

you'd have a horrible metallic taste in your mouth – a
sure sign you were blowing up – and there were still
five more ahead of you. With the coaches watching, and
every move being videoed, there was no hiding place.
Also, you'd be doing the test alongside players in similar
positions in the team (in my case, back three players like
Shane and George North), and everyone would want to
smash each other. By the end, there'd be bodies sprawled
everywhere. Knowing what to expect, the staff left the
fire doors in the indoor centre open: boys would crawl
through them to be sick.

I was usually one of the better performers in the Watt
Test, so I knew I was in trouble when, prior to the World
Cup, I was blown away by everyone. I'd just returned to
running after my knee problems, and in my frustration
I'd been going on the piss a lot. In the past, I might have
been able to shake this off. But this time – undercooked
after missing out on the conditioning camp in Poland – I
was absolutely demolished by everyone. It hurt. 'Fucking
hell,' I thought, 'I'm in trouble here.' And I was. If it
hadn't been for the injury to Morgan Stoddart, I'd have
missed out on New Zealand altogether.

As someone who was used to being one of the fittest
there, this was a blow to my pride. Like I said before,
putting in the hours was really important to me. I liked
nothing better than doing 'extras' at the gym or the
dunes, thinking that while I was still working others
might be inside playing Xbox. Not every player was
so conscientious, mind you – although not all of them

needed to be. Sitiveni Sivivatu, for example, would appear to do very little all week but then turn up and beat the opposition on his own. Napolioni Nalaga, who occupied the opposing wing at Clermont, was similar. Nalaga devised his own weights routine. Rather than breaking his exercises down into 'sets' like the rest of us, he'd just do them all in one go. So, for example, he'd do 20 bench presses (instead of four sets of five). Then he'd move onto the next exercise and do the same, and be out of the gym in about 10 minutes.

Generally speaking, South Sea Islanders like Sivi and Napolioni are genetic freaks when it comes to this! Take Salesi Finau, another winger with whom I shared a dressing room. At the Scarlets, we'd each be given our weights programmes to do in pre-season. Salesi was already massive – with the biggest legs I'd ever seen – but at the end of the first week of training, he'd put on 5 kg. I'm not sure I ever managed that in my entire career! They had to stop him from going in the gym after that.

In the summer of 2012, before my second season with Clermont, I decided to get myself into peak condition. I wanted to hit the ground running in France and, after missing the previous Six Nations, was determined to show Rob Howley and co what they were missing. As it happened, my fitness drive coincided with my honeymoon in Malaysia, which we'd postponed as our wedding clashed with the rugby season. Much to the bewilderment of Andrea (and the alarm of airport security staff when they first spotted it on the x-ray machine), I packed a 10 kg weighted vest in my suitcase. Each morning, I'd be up at 6.30, doing beach sprints wearing the vest. Then, in the evening, it was off to the gym for weights. Four hours of training a day for 12 days is probably not how most people spend their honeymoon, admittedly. But I was determined to make my move to Clermont a success.

That said, even I'd concede that you need a break from the gym sometimes. At Clermont, Vern Cotter decided to shake things up by taking us on a military-style boot camp. For three days, we lived in tents in the midst of remote woodland. Each morning at 6 a.m. we'd be woken by the sound of exploding smoke grenades, let off by the ex-French special forces guys in charge. Then it was a full day of army training, wading through streams while carrying logs, things like that. When it was time to eat, it was largely a case of living off the land – which in practice meant killing chickens to put on the barbecue. The prospect of breaking a bird's neck was too much for me, but came as second nature to the South Africans in the group. Others were less comfortable in the great outdoors, though. Regan showed that his mastery of angles didn't extend to camping. He pitched his tent on a slope so spent the night sleeping upside down, like a bat.

At the Ospreys, it was more a case of old-fashioned sweat and hard work, and we had no shortage of grafters. Alun Wyn Jones, as I've already mentioned, had a great appetite for training. Another one was Marty Holah, the ex-All Blacks flanker. He was an absolute animal in the

gym. Nicknamed 'the Chin' because of his liking for chin-
ups, he'd often do them with 80 kgs of weight hanging
from his midriff. His back was enormous: no wonder he
was immovable at the turnover. Everyone wanted to train
like him. Stefan Terblanche, another overseas star and,
like me, a full back, was another great role model. A
total athlete, ripped to shreds, he'd always be last off the
training field, despite being past 30.

I took a lot from Stefan, but generally I gave other
full backs a wide berth. I wouldn't say I hated them
– and now I'm retired I love most of them – but when
I was playing, I avoided socialising with them. It's not
surprising, I suppose. At the end of the day, we were all
competing for the same thing. At the Scarlets, the man in
my sights was Barry Davies, and at the Ospreys, Stefan.
When I was trying to break into the Wales set-up, Kevin
Morgan was the guy I was trying to oust. I'm sure it's
exactly the same for players in other positions. It's hard
to be matey with someone when you're fighting it out for
the same jersey.

That's not to say I didn't have a healthy respect for
other players in my position. As I've already said, I had
a lot of time for Morgan Stoddart. Barry was a brilliant
bloke and player, and someone who was perhaps unlucky
not to feature more for Wales. Towards the end of my
time with the Wales team, I trained alongside Liam
Williams, and you could see the talent he had. I once saw
him trip over some tackle bags as he back-pedalled to
take a high ball. But, even as he fell, he kept his eye on

the ball and took the catch. That impressed me. It was clear he had courage.

By the time I got to Clermont, I was at a different stage of my career, and able to see the situation from the other side. There, they had a fantastic young full back called Jean-Marcellin Buttin, a 21 year old. I'll admit it: he could do things I couldn't do. By that point, my legs were going a bit, as they do in sport, and he was rapid – able to score length-of-the-field tries. At one point they dropped me for him. I'm sure sections of the crowd preferred him, being young and exciting. But when it came to the big games, they'd always pick me. Jean-Marcellin was a bit flaky under the high ball, whereas they knew I'd give them solidity.

It was a strange role-reversal. I didn't feel guilty, but I could empathise with the youngster's frustration. After all, I'd been there myself ten years previously. I also worried that I was impeding his progress as an international player. While I was at Clermont, Jean-Marcellin made his international debut, but he's found further opportunities hard to come by. In some ways, his difficulties are symptomatic of the French system, where it's hard for homegrown talent to flourish because of all the overseas players. These days he's at Bordeaux and playing well – I hope he can push on.

I played against some excellent number 15s in my time, none more so than All Black Mils Muliaina. But to be honest, I didn't generally worry about the opposing full back when I was doing my pre-match analysis. I would look to see if they stepped off their right or left foot, but that would be about it. I couldn't see the point in doing much more: in the heat of battle the player might do the complete opposite of what I was expecting anyway. I preferred just to let the match unfold. If anything, I'd use analysis to look at my own game, reviewing clips to see how I could improve. That's not to say I didn't have a healthy respect for my opponents, especially fleet-footed wingers. I'd wonder what I'd do if I found myself in a one-on-one situation against them. With the best will in the world, it's tough to stop a flying Fijian who can step off either foot.

One opponent I'd dread playing against was Ronan O'Gara. Not because of his running threat, but because of that deadly-accurate spiral kick he'd do into the corners. I'd worry about him moving me around and catching me out of position. The only time we had some joy against 'Rog' and his kicking game was in that Championship decider of 2009. Shaun Edwards came up with the plan of putting two players – myself and Mark Jones – into the zone between the touchline and the five-metre line, leaving the middle of the field open. Every time Rog looked up, he'd see us there. To some extent, that neutralised the threat, although of course he had the last laugh – kicking the drop goal that sealed the Irish Slam.

As a full back, kicking was a big part of my game too, and again something that I put plenty of time and effort into perfecting. The punt downfield was one my specialities, and I also got plenty of change out of the kick chase, something I'd first discovered at Tondu when I'd gathered one of my own up-and-unders and ran on to score. By the time of my recall to the Wales set-up under Warren Gatland, it had become a major weapon in my arsenal.

'Kicking to contest', as it's known, was nothing new. But the kick is usually put in by one player (typically the number 10) and chased by others. Not many successfully chase down their own kicks. The secret is getting the distance right. I've known players lump it 50 m up the field: pointless, as they're never going to get there. 20–30 m is about right. Another common mistake is to wait until you're too close to a defender, thereby making it easy for him to block your progress. Again – if your run is obstructed in any way you won't get there. Ideally, you want to be kicking 5 m from the nearest defender, while on the move, and ready to chase at full tilt.

Getting it right took practice. Once a week, after training, I'd head to the South Wales Police ground in Bridgend with a bag of balls and some cones. I'd measure out two points, 30 metres apart, then launch the kick, chasing it down and leaping above imaginary defenders to gather. I found using the side of my foot, soccer-style, worked best. You didn't want to put the ball up too high – I came to regard the kick as a sort of high chip, as opposed to a traditional up-and-under.

It became one of my trademarks, and by the time of

the 2008 Grand Slam I'd honed it to a fine art. I even earned my own nickname: the 'bomb defuser', or 'bomb squad' (a 'bomb' being rugby slang for a high ball). Up the kick would go, I'd chase and – more often than not – catch, and lay the platform for a fresh attack. The tactic paid off handsomely the following summer in South Africa with the Lions, when I used it to score in our opening match. It helped us out of a sticky situation.

Of course, catching high balls takes courage – you have to be prepared to be taken out. That's where all my early scrapes on the Wildmill Estate paid dividends – all those falls from trees and garages, and generally not giving a shit about my own welfare. I'm not saying I have a high pain threshold – quite the opposite in fact – but I don't tend to worry about the pain until it actually happens. The only time I felt a bit put off was after an incident for the Ospreys against Perpignan, where I landed badly and turned my ankle.

One of the few people who worked out how to stop the kick chase was Gethin Jenkins. Gethin and I spent a lot of time together in the Wales camp, and he used his insider knowledge to good effect when the Ospreys played the Blues. I'd set off after a kick, only to find the considerable frame of 'Melon' blocking my progress. As well as being a big lump, he's also deceptively quick, and I'd struggle to get round him before the ball landed.

Other players who are good practitioners of the technique include Ireland's Rob Kearney and our very own

Dan Biggar, whose salmon-like leaps became a feature of the 2015 World Cup. Sadly, these days, with referees cracking down on making contact with players in the air, I fear it may be a dying art. If I was starting out now, I'm not sure it would be such an important facet of my game.

*****

I've stopped playing now, but I'm still a fitness nut, getting up at 6 a.m. to train. I certainly want to stay involved with the strength and conditioning side of rugby in the future. One of my jobs since I retired has been doing personal training sessions for a few private clients. Sometimes I'll take them to the dunes at Merthyr Mawr, where I started out. They can't pull the wool over my eyes when we're there: after 20 years of running up and down them, I know every inch of those slopes. I can tell exactly how hard they're working.

For me, the place stirs strangely pleasurable memories. I associate those dunes with the sweat and sacrifice which took me to the top of my game.

CHAPTER 14

Jerry

Every time I hear the electric gates opening in my driveway, it's the same, even now. I'll stop what I'm doing for a moment and look up, half expecting Jerry Collins to walk through them, looking the worse for wear.

For two years, during the period when Jerry and I were teammates at the Ospreys, it was a sight I became used to. The big man had his own house, you understand, but at weekends, to all intents and purposes, he'd live at mine. Or at least he'd crash there when he wasn't out enjoying himself. He wasn't really one to follow normal rules, you see.

Jerry and I became the best of friends, but our first meeting was less amicable. It happened moments after I ran onto the field at the Millennium Stadium to make my Wales debut. I think it was actually my first touch of the ball in international rugby. It didn't last long. Within about 10 seconds I was flat on my back, put there by the scary-looking All Black flanker with the bleached-blonde hair. He patted my head, not unaffectionately: 'Next time step, bro,' he said, and ran off to rejoin the fray. I may have mentioned it already, but they won 45-3.

We never crossed paths again in international rugby. He finished playing for New Zealand in 2007, with 48 caps to his name, before leaving the land of the white cloud to join Toulon. A year later he signed a two-year deal with the Ospreys, and the Liberty Stadium side had another star in its ranks.

Jerry may have died at 34, but he packed more into his life than most 80 year olds have managed to. He was fearsome on the field, but impossible to dislike off it; unconcerned by money, and generous to a fault. I'd always liked South Seas Islanders, with their 'work hard, play hard' philosophy of life. 'JC' fitted that mould, and then some. I liked to think that I enjoyed life, but he took that attitude to a different level.

Although he did own a car, he had lifts or taxis everywhere. On Sundays (his main time for drinking), he'd hire a cab for the day. Not for him the bright lights of Swansea or Cardiff, though. Instead he'd get the driver to take him to the rugby club in, say, Hirwaun, where he'd spend the day having a few pints with the locals. He'd generally be dressed in shorts, a vest and flip-flops: he didn't really do smart.

We did persuade him to make the effort now and then. One time – for a change – I organised a night out in Bristol, together with my mates Jonathan Stoker and Mark Florence. Jerry had splashed out and bought himself a shirt, some jeans and a decent pair of shoes. We hired a limo to take us. We'd picked up the last of the boys from Cardiff and were heading towards the M4, passing through the suburb of Ely, when Jerry asked the driver to stop at this random pub. 'This is my local,' he said – explaining that he'd been drinking there on his day off – and wanted to go in and say hello. He produced a bag containing his usual garb – shorts, vest, flip-flops – and changed, explaining that the regulars would never recognise him otherwise. Inside, he insisted on buying everyone a Jägerbomb... before changing back into his smart gear for the onward journey to Bristol.

That night, or another like it, ended in surreal fashion. We'd left the nightclub late, so late it was daylight as we walked back to our hotel. A rubbish truck was doing its rounds and Jerry – who'd once been a bin-man in his home town of Wellington – decided he wanted to help. The next thing I knew he was on the back of the truck, getting off to collect the rubbish bags. The crew didn't mind – they even let me sit up front next to the driver, who happened to be Welsh. I bumped into him recently and he reminded me of the incident.

Our favourite haunt was The Three Golden Cups in Southerndown. Each week 'Sunday club' would convene, starting at midday. It would be Jerry, me, Scott Baldwin – the Wales hooker – and my mates Jonathan Stoker, Rory Pitman and Jamie Docherty. We'd load up the jukebox, get stuck into the Jägerbombs and shoot some pool, before emerging, steaming, around 8 p.m. The festivities would continue till the small hours at my place – usually to the strains of 'I Don't Like Mondays' by the Boomtown

Rats on the sound system. A few hours later I'd wake up, feeling shit, to the scent of omelettes cooking downstairs. After he'd eaten and smoked a couple of fags, Jerry would be good to go: I'd be dying. One Monday morning I was sick in the car en route to training. I don't think I made it to work that day.

Despite being seemingly hangover-proof, JC still went to some lengths to maintain the image of clean living. Before we got to the ground, he'd tell me to pull over at a newsagent's so he could buy a paper: he'd then fold it up and carry it under his arm into training. He said it made him look businesslike. To be fair, he always looked the same, hung-over or not... unless, that is, you got up close, and smelled the vodka emanating from his pores.

JC usually looked the part too, but not necessarily because he'd done his laundry. One time – having forgotten or lost his training gear – he made me stop at a sports shop in Bridgend. Inside, he bought a complete set of Ospreys replica kit and some rugby boots. Most people wouldn't get away with such antics, but he always trained as well as anyone. It helped that he kept himself extremely fit, doing extra boxing sessions in the week to supplement the rugby.

On the field he had a tremendous influence, particularly in the 2010 league-winning season. His reputation for hard tackling (immortalised in Wales by the huge hit he put in on Colin Charvis in 2002), was well justified. To use a term from the World Wrestling

Federation, he wanted to 'suplex' everyone. Together with his fellow All Blacks Marty Holah and Filo Tiatia (Filo usually coming off the bench), he was part of a formidable and frightening back-row trio. I certainly wouldn't have wanted to be on the opposing side.

*****

I stayed in touch with JC after he left Wales. He returned from his new club in Japan for my wedding, hiring a cab from Heathrow to the venue in Mid Wales, before paying for everyone's dinner the night before the ceremony. I'd asked him to be an usher, but naturally he'd failed to provide any suit measurements, despite me nagging him for five weeks. In the end, he bought at suit at the airport and still turned up looking sharp, despite his borrowed shoes being a few sizes too big.

Andrea and I were married at the Glanusk Estate in Mid Wales, home of the Legge-Bourke family After Jerry died, Tiggy Legge-Bourke (the former nanny of Princes William and Harry), wrote us a lovely letter describing how JC – who'd been staying at her B & B nearby – had played rugby for hours in the garden with her kids. She also told a funny story about walking into the kitchen one morning to find the big man clad only in a hand towel, which must have been an unusual sight in the genteel surroundings of a Mid Wales country estate.

The outlandish adventures continued abroad. In Japan,

Jerry made the news after being chased around the block by some sword-wielding members of the Brazilian mafia. He told me they'd confused him with a Tongan rugby player with whom they'd recently had an altercation. He got himself arrested for his own safety and was flown out of the country. Next, he spent a year in Canada, working as a security guard at a residential centre for oil-riggers during their inshore rest periods.

Finally, in 2014, he found himself back in New Zealand, at the wedding of his best mate Chris Masoe, where he bumped into ex-Wallaby back row Rocky Elsom. Rocky was player-coach at Narbonne in the French Second Division. They were struggling, and in danger of relegation. To make matters worse he (Rocky) was injured and the club needed a replacement: did Jerry fancy coming out of retirement? And so it came to pass that he signed for Narbonne as a so called 'medical joker' (injury cover, to you and me) in January 2015.

This being JC, it wasn't a low-key return. By all accounts, he more or less single-handedly saved Narbonne from the drop, picking up three man-of-the-match awards in eight games and scoring half a dozen tries. The club offered him a three-year deal, and the next stage was to fly Alana, his Canadian partner – who'd recently given birth to their first child – out to join him.

I last saw him in the summer of 2015, the day before he was due to fly to Canada to collect his family. We met in Narbonne. I walked into the clubhouse to find him in an ice bath, fag in mouth. He invited me to go upstairs and introduce myself to the guys in charge, including Elsom and Club President Anthony Hill (who I'd never met), as he'd been speaking to them about hiring me as a kicking consultant. After he got dressed, we hopped in the car and drove to Toulouse, where Sivivatu, by this time playing at Castres, joined us. We convened at the bar of Trevor Brennan, the ex-Ireland and Toulouse forward, who joined us for a drink. I was due to fly out at 5 p.m. the following day, JC at nine in the morning. It was a fair bender. The next morning, we'd completely forgotten where we'd parked the hire car, which was a bit of a problem since it contained our bags and travel documents. So, we got a cab and had the driver take us round the city. I was holding the key fob out of the open window, repeatedly pressing 'unlock' in the hope we'd see some tell-tale flashing lights. Eventually, we did. We retrieved the bags and hightailed it to the airport, arriving with little time to spare. Jerry smoked a final fag and bade me goodbye. A few days later he sent me a short text: 'That was a hell of a night, you big c**t.'

I've never deleted that message.

*****

Less than a week later, on the morning of 5 June, I awoke to news I could barely comprehend: Jerry had died in a car crash. It had been the middle of the night, and Alana was driving. For some reason she'd lost control of the car and it had ploughed into the path of a bus, killing her and Jerry, who'd been in the back, instantly. A post mortem found no alcohol in Alana's bloodstream – investigators say it was simply a tragic accident. Ayla, their three month old daughter, was taken to hospital with critical brain injuries. When the emergency services arrived, they found her underneath her father: it appeared he'd thrown his body over her in the instants before the impact.

There was no hesitation about flying out to New Zealand for the funeral. I arrived at the Collins family home in Porirua – a suburb of Wellington – to find an enormous pile of shoes in the hallway (mine later vanished – 'Samoan kids for you,' joked one of the Samoans). All Black stars of past and present – from Jonah Lomu to Sonny Bill Williams – were among the ordinary people who'd come to pay their respects.

Jerry was lying upstairs. Our mutual friend Chris Masoe offered to take me up to see him. 'If you start crying, I'll give you a 'buka',' he said, 'buka' being a local term for a slap. We walked into the room. Jerry was lying in an open coffin, resplendent in his All Blacks suit. He looked like he was about to sit up and say hello. By his side sat his mother, crying her eyes out. She stayed with him the whole time, while different visitors came and went. Despite Chris' warning, I couldn't stop the tears. But I composed myself enough to sit down alongside my pal and talk to him for a while. Eventually, the time came to leave him with his mum.

Downstairs in the garage, everyone was drinking and telling stories about JC. His dad Frank, a very tough man (legend had it he'd once made Jerry stand up and start walking on a broken leg), asked each of us to stand up and explain to the gathering how we knew his son. I also presented him with a photo album of Jerry's time in Wales. Later, to my great honour, I was asked to be one of the pallbearers at the funeral.

The next morning, still jet-lagged, I got up at 5 a.m. and went to a 24-hour gym near the hotel. Chris Masoe and his wife were coming to pick me up at midday. But after the gym, instead of my usual protein shake, I downed a bottle of wine in the room. After all, JC wouldn't want me turning up sober for his funeral.

I've seen some hakas in my time – facing the full might of the All Blacks' war dance in front of thousands at the Millennium Stadium – but I'll never forget the one performed by schoolchildren as we carried Jerry's coffin from the memorial hall. I was shaking with emotion: God knows how the other pallbearers felt. They were all Polynesian: my former Ospreys teammate Filo Tiatia was there, along with ex-London Irish player Seilala Mapusua, Chris Masoe, Ma'a Nonu and Tana Umaga – Jerry's cousin.

According to the local custom, the six of us helped to shovel the earth in over our friend after we'd laid him the ground. Then we poured vodka, his favourite tipple, on top. Fittingly, a pub crawl followed. We took his passport with us, and poured some drink over his photo every time someone got a round. If the big man was looking down, he'd have enjoyed that.

I've stayed in touch with his family. In 2016, I visited his grave during a holiday to New Zealand with Andrea, and met up with his sisters, Brenda and Helen (both of whom share their brother's fun-loving approach to life). I've also been to see Ayla in Canada, where she's being looked after by her grandparents, Darrell and Ruth, and Alana's sisters, Brenna and Nora. The doctors say she'll continue to need medical support, but she has a fantastic family network around her. Back here in Wales, we've tried to do our bit to help. A few months after the funeral, the other members of the 'Fab Four' and I held a fundraising dinner at the Liberty Stadium, raising £20,000. With her family around her, and the help of well-wishers around the world, I'm sure Ayla's future will be secure.

Although losing Jerry was a tragedy, I'm so glad I knew him. He was an infectious character, true to himself, and one of the most fun people you could hope to meet. I guess he was inspiration, too: a walking lesson about the importance of enjoying life, and making the most of every moment.

CHAPTER 15

Survivor

Careers in professional sport, particularly those in rugby, are short. Mine had lasted a little over 12 years. Even if, like me, you've been lucky enough to reach the top of your game, that won't give you enough money to retire on – especially if, like me, you've sometimes been a little loose with your spending.

As I've already described, being a retired ex-pro can be a lonely place, particularly if you haven't got any qualifications to fall back on. The hangers-on who'd seemed so interested in Lee Byrne when his stock was high were suddenly nowhere to be seen. I remember the reaction of my agent at the time when I rang him to say I'd be retiring from the Dragons: 'You mean you won't be seeing out your contract?' My premature exit meant he'd miss out on his commission. It was clear where his priorities lay: my welfare was not uppermost on the list.

At moments like this, you look to your wider support networks to kick in. In Wales, we have the Welsh Rugby Players Association, the WRPA. Sadly, I found them to be absolutely useless. As a player, you pay £10 a month into their coffers to be a member, but – as far as I was

concerned – when I needed them they were nowhere
to be seen. It's quite a contrast with the organisation's
English counterpart, the RPA, which arranges work
placements for its members with city firms like
PricewaterhouseCoopers. For someone like me who's
done well out of the game financially, maybe their support
isn't so crucial. But for your average regional player, who
makes perhaps £30–40,000 a year from rugby, having a
players' union to help ease the transition to life outside
the game is, I believe, vitally important. Hopefully Andries
Pretorius, the former Wales player who has now taken
over at the WRPA, can help improve things.

For me, finding my way in this new world was
bewildering. To start with, I seemed to spend all my time
in meetings, many of which proved pointless. There was
lots of talk, but very little in the way of actual offers.
Early on, I was offered some sales work by a photocopiers
company called Clarity, who'd been one of the Ospreys'
main sponsors. Don't get me wrong, I was grateful to
them for asking, and the money was good – but I couldn't
help but feel a certain reluctance. I wondered what people
would make of it: a former British Lion turned photocopier
salesman.

Naturally, I thought rugby might be a good bet for me.
At one point, I was in the frame to coach Risca. Next,
Glynneath were interested, but then I had an apologetic
call from Max Boyce to say they'd offered the job to the
ex-Neath player Patrick Horgan instead. A contact at the
Dragons told me Monmouth Comprehensive School were

looking for a rugby coach, and I thought working there might give me a foot in the door at the nearby private school, with whom the WRU were looking to build a closer relationship. But when I met with John Bevan, the Wales and Lions legend and head of rugby at Monmouth School, it became clear there was no vacancy. It wasn't the right time for me anyway: I was struggling with depression and hadn't yet had help. I did a day at Monmouth Comp and never went back, which no doubt let a few people down.

Another job offer, as backs coach with Bridgend RFC, didn't work out. I'd also tried, and failed, to find work in the professional tier of the game. It was frustrating, but I think my experience reflects a wider 'brain drain' afflicting Welsh rugby. All too often, retired players don't get the opportunity to impart their knowledge to the next generation. Yes, I understand that there's a process to be followed and coaching badges to be obtained. I also accept that a great player doesn't necessarily make a great coach. But surely the regions should be doing more to tap into the collective knowledge of those who've played at the highest level? After all, look at the impact my old Wales teammate Stephen Jones has had with the Scarlets. Sadly, Stephen seems to be the exception rather than rule: for many of us ex-internationals, making the transition from the field to the coaching box seems harder than it ought to be.

My luck changed following a meeting with Gerald McCarthy, a good friend of mine. Gerald told me about a new rugby-league franchise starting up in Merthyr that would in time, it was hoped, achieve great things. In a nod to the area's industrial heritage, the new team was to be called the 'South Wales Ironmen', and would play at a redeveloped home ground of Wern Park. I met the club's owners, who asked me if I wanted to become Director of Rugby.

It wasn't hard to say 'yes.' Ever since my days with the Bridgend Blue Bulls, I'd had an affinity with the 13-man code. Given the unhappy history of the game in Wales (which most recently saw the Celtic Crusaders reach the Super League before folding), the cynics predicted more failure. But at the time, it was the chance to be in at the start of a new and exciting adventure.

My ambition to become a Strength and Conditioning Coach had been thwarted by the realisation I'd have to go to college to get a qualification – not an option with bills to pay. But my new opportunity gave me the chance to put some of my knowledge into action, by preparing the pre-season fitness programmes for our new squad. On the day of our first home fixture, against Whitehaven in the league, I had butterflies in my stomach. Given the chance, I'd have run onto the field myself.

Sadly, the owners of the club ran into financial problems and the project went under. But it wasn't a completely wasted exercise: one of our sponsors at the club was Dribuild, a growing construction and refurbishment company, with a portfolio of blue-chip clients across the UK, and I've been doing some work with them. The three directors – Matt Tyler, Mike Holt and Dave Kipling – are great guys: down to earth and very much men of their word. We hit it off straight away. Matt, Mike and Dave have built Dribuild up from nothing into a company turning over tens of millions. According to the *Financial Times*, it's one of the fastest-growing businesses in Europe. As Regional Development Manager, my job is to help the company grow its client base in Wales. Basically it involves meeting movers and shakers in the sector and trying to win new contracts. In a funny way, doing a deal gives me a similar buzz to scoring a try: like I've done my bit to help the team achieve its goal.

I love working for Dribuild – it's given me a new lease of life. I'd like to put on record my thanks to Matt, Mike and Dave for the faith they've shown in me. Their offer of work came a vital time: without it, I may have continued on the depressive spiral I'd entered after quitting rugby. If they sacked me tomorrow, I'd still shake them by the hand. And it turns out I'm not the only sportsman connected to the company. Peter Trego, the Somerset county cricketer, is sponsored by them and – as I discovered during a recent business trip to Abu Dhabi with him – shares my passion for fitness. Keen to find a way to keep the blood flowing during our seven-hour flight, we decided to do some press-ups: 350, to be precise. Every hour, we'd get up and head to the back of the plane where we'd knock off 50, our fellow-passengers stepping over us en route to the toilet. Then it was back to our seats for some more wine. A boozer and a body-builder: Peter's very much a man after my own heart!

Doing the Myers-Briggs test, overseen by consultant Mark Wilcox, also focused my mind. Mark observed I'd been approaching working life like a magpie, flitting between any shiny objects that fell into my path, but unable to settle for any of them. What I needed was a plan. After nine hours of testing, Mark concluded that a career spent behind a desk was not for me. Better, he said, to diversify. He drew a pie chart on the whiteboard, dividing it into different sections according to my interests: rugby, media, business and so on. To be fair, he was spot on. I've adopted the 'lots of little jobs' approach ever since, becoming – in rugby parlance – a utility player.

The media has become an important part of the pie. Initially I found TV difficult, after suffering a bit of a panic attack one time before appearing on Sky. But I really enjoy radio, and regularly cover games for BBC Wales. On a recent trip to Newcastle to commentate on a European tie, I found myself sitting next to a face from the past: Phil Steele – my old teacher from St Mary's. As you may know, Phil's fought his own battle with depression, and it was interesting to swap stories with him after the game. It's funny how things work out. Years after 'Mr Stel' had first given me my chance alongside the big kids at St Mary's, here I was working alongside him. It felt like I'd come full circle.

When I first retired, I wasn't actually a huge watcher of rugby in my spare time. I suppose that was partly because there was still a big part of me that would have liked to still be playing. Even then, I did make an exception for the international games, and I enjoyed watching Super Rugby. As we saw on the recent Lions tour, the speed and skill levels on show there are at a different level – how the game should be played, in my opinion. It's how I like to think I played myself.

Without wishing to sound like some bore from the 70s, I do think the Wales team I played in was more exciting than today's. With the players we had – the likes of Shane, Henson, Hooky and Stephen Jones – I felt like we really knew how to entertain. I'm not sure that's the case now, even though there's no shortage of talent in the Welsh set-up. Having said that, I guess most players would say their era was the best one!

So what have I got to show for my career in rugby? Not as much as you might think, and certainly not enough to sit back and never work again. I made a lot of money when my profile was high, and I'd definitely be a richer man if I'd invested it shrewdly. But I was pretty extravagant with my cash back in those days. One time, I spent £2,500 on a table for my mate Carl Tozer and me at this posh club in London. Factor in drinks, and I reckon the night set me back about £5,000. Which would have been alright if we hadn't been sitting behind a pillar the whole time. £5,000 to sit behind a pillar. Still, I'm sure we enjoyed ourselves.

Then there was the time when, during a party at my house, I noticed a stash of notes on top of the wardrobe. I assumed it was gambling winnings. For a laugh, I grabbed the notes and threw them in the air, watching them settle around the revellers. I suppose that story says plenty about my attitude to money at that time.

The thing is, when it comes down to it, despite all the high times I've had – all the cars, the girls, the booze and the big nights – I'm still a Wildmill boy at heart. If it all vanished tomorrow and I ended up living in a one-bedroom flat, I'd be happy. And I certainly don't begrudge a penny of the thousands I spent having a good time with my mates from home. One of the things I always wanted to do was to take them on the journey with me. I'm so glad I was able to do that.

I suppose my big earning days are behind me now. But if there's one moral I can draw from my life and career, it's that I'm a survivor: I'll find a way. Of course, it helps that I've got a great family behind me. There's my mum and dad, who scrimped and saved to give me opportunities when I was kid, and of course my wife, Andrea. To her I owe a special debt of gratitude. She's had to put up with a lot: two years with me in a different country, my Wales disappointments, the stress of my career-ending injury and all the problems that followed. I treated her very badly during that time, in lots of ways. I won't go into all the details, but suffice to say she's had a lot to put up with. How she didn't leave me I don't know, but I'm eternally grateful she didn't. She's the best thing that's ever happened to me.

As the dust settles on my career, I feel proud of what I achieved. To be a Grand Slam winner, a British and Irish Lion, a Heineken Cup finalist and a three-times Pro12 champion – it's certainly more than I dared dream of when I was getting £25 per win at Bridgend Athletic. Along the way I've met some great people, and had some unforgettable experiences.

Who knows what will come next? But whatever lies ahead, at least I realised the ambition of the teenager sitting on his bed all those years ago: to buy his mum and dad a nicer house. I fulfilled that dream... and many more I could never have imagined.

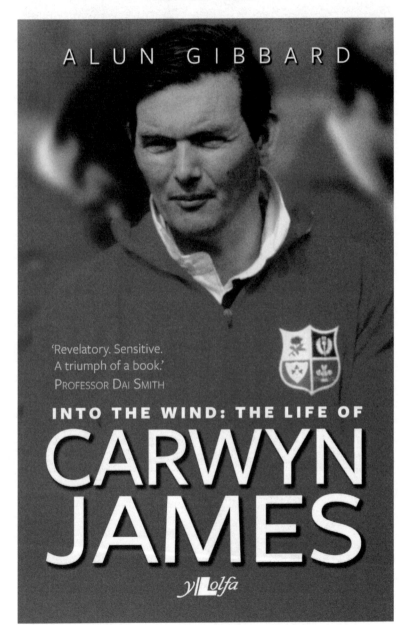

ALUN GIBBARD

'Revelatory. Sensitive.
A triumph of a book.'
PROFESSOR DAI SMITH

INTO THE WIND: THE LIFE OF

CARWYN
JAMES

yLolfa

£14.99

IAN GOUGH

'Straight talking about the highs and lows of Welsh rugby'

GOUGHY
A TOUGH LOCK TO CRACK

y Lolfa

£9.99

JJ Williams

the life and times of a rugby legend

JJ Williams with Peter Jackson

y Lolfa

£14.99

The Byrne Identity is just one of a whole range of publications from Y Lolfa. For a full list of books currently in print, send now for your free copy of our new full-colour catalogue. Or simply surf into our website

www.ylolfa.com

for secure on-line ordering.

TALYBONT CEREDIGION CYMRU SY24 5HE
e-mail ylolfa@ylolfa.com
website www.ylolfa.com
phone (01970) 832 304
fax 832 782

Ask for a print quote!
01970 832 304